The Global Jukebox

Popular music is with us constantly. It is part of our everyday environment in McLuhan's 'Global Village' and is now amongst the most universal means of communication.

The Global Jukebox is the first comprehensive study of the international music industry at a time of great change, as the entertainment industry acknowledges its ever growing global audience. It provides an international overview of the music business and its future prospects in the global marketplace.

As record companies are swallowed up by massive multimedia empires Robert Burnett examines the relationship between local and global cultures and between concentration of ownership (the 'Big Six' multinational corporations Time Warner, Sony, Philips, Bertelsmann, Thorn–EMI and Matsushita) and the impact of subsequent economic imperatives on music production and consumption. Other topics include definitions of popular music; current industry developments; the new media technologies – digitalization, satellite broadcasting and 'virtual music stores' ɔ᷈ the Internet; and the role of the largest and single most important m   r commercial music, the United States.

The Global Jukebox not only illuminates the workir   porary entertainment industries, it captures the d᷈   production of musical culture between the trar   erates, the independent music companies ar   ntial reading for anyone studying popular music.

Robert Burnett is Head of Media and Communi   Studies at the University of Karlstad, Sweden. He has published extensively on popular music, the music industry and popular culture.

Communication and Society
General Editor: James Curran

The Global Jukebox

The international music industry

Robert Burnett

London and New York

First published 1996
by Routledge
11 New Fetter Lane, London EC4P 4EE

Simultaneously published in the USA and Canada
by Routledge
29 West 35th Street, New York, NY 10001

Typeset in Times by
Florencetype Ltd, Stoodleigh, Devon

Printed and bound in Great Britain by
Clays Ltd, St Ives plc

British Library Cataloguing in Publication Data
A catalogue record for this book is available from
the British Library

Library of Congress Cataloguing in Publication Data
A catalogue record for this book has been requested

ISBN 0–415–09275–2
      0–415–09276–0 (pbk)

For my children,
Sara and Jonatan

Contents

Figures

Tables

Acknowledgements

This book reflects my personal history as a Canadian schooled on the writings of Harold Innis, Marshall McLuhan and Dallas Smythe. I have had the good fortune of living most of my adult life in Europe where I have been exposed to other theoretical traditions. I like to think this combination is reflected in my work.

The ideas in this book are, for the most part, mine but they are based on the writings of those before me. I also want to acknowledge the input of friends and colleagues who, over the years, have spent hours with me discussing the music. As the song goes, you know who you are!

This manuscript and my work before it has also benefited immensely from the careful comments of James Curran, Johan Fornäs, Simon Frith, Paul Hirsch, Krister Malm, Denis McQuail, Richard Peterson, Bo Reimer, Keith Roe, Even Ruud, John Shepherd, Roger Wallis and Robert Weber. (I have been fortunate!)

I also want to thank my informants in the music business, most of whom prefer to remain anonymous, who were gracious enough to try to answer my often silly questions.

An acknowledgement is also due to the students of media and communication studies I have had the pleasure to teach in Canada, Norway, Sweden and Zimbabwe.

A big thanks is due to all my friends and colleagues involved in the International Association for the Study of Popular Music for providing an international forum for the exchange of ideas. Please, if you have any thoughts to discuss send me an e-mail. My address is Robert.Burnett@hks.se

Most of all, thanks to my family who make it all worthwhile.

Robert Burnett
Sjöstad, Sweden

Chapter 1

Introduction

Popular music is with us constantly, it is part of our everyday environment, and increasingly part of the aural or sonic soundscape that surrounds us. Not only do we listen to music in our homes and at concerts, but also as a background in cars, bars, aeroplanes, restaurants and shopping malls. Tagg (1982: 37) has estimated that the 'average Westerner's brain probably spends around twenty five per cent of its lifetime registering, monitoring and decoding' popular music. Chambers (1982: 19) has noted that popular music is 'one of the more powerful expressions of the "culture industry"' worldwide. Robinson (1986: 33), goes as far as to claim that popular music 'is the only truly universal mass medium'. Certainly most people would agree with Bradley's (1981: 205) observation that 'music speaks a universal language of emotions'. Popular music is now the lingua franca for a large segment of the world's youth population. It's probably fair to say that music is the most universal means of communication we now have, instantly traversing language and other cultural barriers in a way that academics rarely understand.

Indeed, whereas consumption of other media products is often limited by geographical availability and consumer income, almost anyone anywhere can listen to popular music, often regardless of whether they want to or not. Most of us at one time or another have felt pursued by music itself. In this respect popular music is certainly the most global aspect of our 'global village'.

It was a Canadian, the late Marshall McLuhan, who called the world a 'global village' created by the homogenizing effects of the universal availability of new electronic technologies. Since he long ago coined the phrase our world has shrunk even further and our horizons have grown wider through new media technologies such as computers, digitalization, video cassettes, satellite broadcasting and cable television. The evolution of technology and the proliferation of global cultural products have had many effects, not the least of which is the fact that the 'stars' of the contemporary entertainment industry are increasingly catering to an international audience that is constantly growing. McLuhan was not thinking of popular music when he coined his now famous phrase, though he might well have been. Today, we are all listening to the *global jukebox*.

In 1994 more than 90 per cent of the gross sales of recorded music worldwide came from albums, singles and music videos owned or distributed by one of six multinational corporations: Time Warner, Sony, Philips, Bertelsmann, Thorn–EMI and Matsushita. Some day soon, the Big Six expect to transmit albums directly into our homes. We will no longer have to visit the record store to buy prerecorded music. The record shops of today may be replaced by 'virtual music shops' on the Internet.

This is something that the music industry is well aware of. The director general of the branch organization, the International Federation of Phonogram and Videogram Producers, recently commented:

> We know, at some time in the future, recorded music will be widely available on-line, interactively, and as a major part of multimedia products; but at present we rely almost exclusively on retailers for the revenue which drives the industry. Our challenge, in terms of developing rights for producers, is how to get from here to there, with an industry intact.
>
> (IFPI, 1995)

The transnationals are intent on keeping control of the music business. 'One of the definitions of a major record company is that you are in the distribution business', said an industry executive. 'We don't simply want to be providers of content to someone else's electronic delivery system. Why would we empower someone else to do this?' (*Details*, 1994).

Roughly speaking, it costs a major label about one dollar to manufacture and package a CD, and another dollar for distribution. Royalties to the artist and songwriter average between one and two dollars per CD. Retailers then add about five dollars to the cost of each CD. Clearly in this equation the major labels are making big money. Now if the Big Six could download their products into our homes, they could reduce their manufacturing and distribution costs as well as eliminate the retailer from the picture. They would make more money and we, the consumers, theoretically might pay less per album. While nobody knows exactly how music, film and information will be delivered into our homes, it is only a matter of years before it starts happening on a major scale.

Popular music is also a phenomenon of increasingly worldwide significance. The international music industry based on the production and sales of phonograms (records, cassettes, mini and compact discs) had an annual turnover in 1994 of $33 billion US worldwide (IFPI, 1995). The industry's products have wide-ranging effects on our acoustical environment, either directly or with the assistance of other forms of mass communication. Phonograms are potent and omnipresent carriers of culture and agents of socialization for whole generations of youth.

Academic research has traditionally shown little systematic interest in popular music. The study of popular music as well as popular culture in general has rarely been considered a serious academic pursuit. Consequently, because of academic neglect, there are gaps in our knowledge about most aspects of popular music. There is still little recognition that music is possibly a much more important component of youth experience with mass media than television, for instance, which has been the subject of intense and wide-ranging research for decades. This lack of interest in popular music by the academy is strongly contrasted by the enthusiasm shown by non-academics. The problem is that most works on popular music and the music industry simply offer a fan's account of the major performers or the most popular songs, although there are also a number of serious works including biographies of major figures, considerations of aspects of the music business or analyses of various styles. None of these, however, give a coherent picture of both the industry and the commercial factors that lie behind the music.

Fortunately the lack of interest on behalf of the academy appears to be changing. Blumler (1985) has criticized the mainstream literature for its continuous focus on the medium of television at the exclusion of all else, while Ewen (1983: 223) suggests that rock 'n' roll is a 'vital resource for studying media in society'. In an important editorial epilogue, Chaffee (1985) further suggests that 'popular music is perhaps the most international mode of communication'. In recent years important academic journals have all published special issues on popular music and a new journal, *Popular Music*, was started. In spite of these positive developments there clearly remains much work to be done.

Seen from a historical perspective, popular music has played an important role in distributing 'America's' myths, dreams and ideals around the world (Frith, 1981). The music industry has also at least partially provided the foundation for many of today's transnational, diversified communication conglomerates. Thus, despite the continuous introduction of new forms of entertainment and communications technology, the music industry remains an important component of the expanding information and entertainment sector. It is especially important to remember that popular music has developed as a commodity which is produced, distributed and consumed under market conditions that inevitably influence the types of phonograms made, who make them, and how they are distributed to the public.

Before the Second World War, the American and British music industries remained essentially domestically based and oriented. Practically all revenues came from the domestic market. Anglo-American music was sold abroad but the resulting revenues hardly compared to what the respective domestic markets yielded. Foreign revenue was simply an added increment, extra profit upon which American and British music companies did not depend. The foreign markets did not warrant enough attention to force companies to modify significantly the music to suit tastes abroad, or induce the companies to maintain elaborate overseas organizations (Gronow, 1983). Today the situation is very different, the American and British music industries now derive over half of their incomes from foreign markets. Of course, some companies exist on revenues derived predominantly from the domestic market, but for the industry as a whole, the foreign market has become very important.

As we near the magic year 2000 one thing is increasingly clear, the cultural economy, at least, is becoming globally integrated. This globalization has been defined by Giddens (1990: 64) as 'the intensification of worldwide social relations which link distant localities in such a way that local happenings are shaped by events occurring many miles away and vice versa'. Globalization in this study refers to the organization, distribution and consumption of cultural products on a global scale. This is particularly evident in the media entertainment industries, especially film, television and music.

Penetration of the world market by the predominantly transnational industry has generated changes in policy and structure worldwide, changes which have important implications for the production, content and marketing of popular music. The economic base of the transnational industry has clearly expanded and the related drive to secure world markets has provoked clearly detectable reactions in some countries.

Although it is impossible to accurately measure, it has been estimated that in the 1990s, American mass media products account for 75 per cent of broadcast and basic cable television revenues worldwide. Some 55 per cent of all film screenings and 55 per cent of all home video rentals worldwide are American materials. American phonograms account for over half of world recording revenues. American books make up 35 per cent of the book market worldwide (Bernstein, 1990: 57). Even if it is no longer the case that the 'media are American' (Tunstall, 1977) the contents appear to remain so to a great extent.

Reviewing most mass communications literature from the 1970s and early 1980s one finds that terms like 'media imperialism' and 'cultural imperialism' are frequently used to sum up the domination of the international news and entertainment fields by American companies. With rare exception, studies of international media simply traced the now familiar story of American domination in publishing, films, television shows and music. This is no longer the case, with takeovers, fusions and mergers in the American publishing, film and music industries by European and Japanese firms becoming a regular occurrence in recent years. During the past decade, the United States lost its sole dominance as the owner and producer of mass communications around the world. The new globalization of ownership of mass media content, production and technology has major implications for audience definitions and theories about who controls these media, for what purposes, and with what effects. Some of the questions that need to be asked are:

- What are the driving forces behind media expansion and concentration?
- What does media concentration mean for diversity and innovation of media content?
- Can there be room for cultural and musical diversity in these times of instant access digital technologies dedicated to pumping the same sounds and images across the entire western popular culture market?

Change, or at least the appearance of change, is vital to the dynamic nature of the entertainment industry. Consumer interests have limited lifespans. The same old products offered again and again inevitably results in declining audiences. The dilemma is that basic entertainment does not change that much. How the entertainment is packaged and delivered is the real subject of change. Just think of all the recording artists who have had their entire musical output reduced to a packaged set of CDs less than the size of a box of corn flakes! The industry struggles to discover new methods of repackaging our entertainment to make it appear novel and unique, although the content often remains the same. This need for change plunges the entertainment industries into high risk ventures. The potentials for hugh payoffs are accompanied by the possibilities of economic disasters. While profits from Spielberg's movie *Jurassic Park* and its accompanying merchandising exceeded a billion dollars worldwide, other movies lose millions of dollars. Michael Jackson's *Thriller* album sold over 40 million copies and almost singlehandedly revived lagging sales across the music industry in the mid-1980s. His follow up albums *Bad* and *Dangerous* have only sold a quarter of what *Thriller* did and have made much less profit for his record label, Sony, than anticipated. Success and failure are relative terms.

Thus, in this study I will suggest that economic imperatives have strongly determined the production and consumption of popular music. In fact, a major argument of this study is the problem of uncertainty and the industry's attempt to overcome it. Uncertainty is the permanent condition of the cultural industries, as it is of much of the entire business world. As Gitlin (1985: 14) points out: 'As soon as capital pays its lip service to risk (for which profit is its just reward), it gets busy trying to minimize it. "The marketplace", the intended recipient of the product, is an abstraction and an imperfect guide. It cannot tell the anxious executive what to do.' Therefore, the music industry, like others, constantly tries to develop new ways to control both supply and demand. The system of production attempts to smooth the process of supply. The system of consumption seeks to ensure that demand is of a sort the companies are set up to satisfy.

The purpose of this study is threefold. The first is to show that popular music is an important and certainly neglected area of research within the literature of media and communication studies. The second is to describe and characterize the contemporary popular music industry and explain its role within the increasingly global entertainment industry. The third and most important is to illuminate and analyse some of the factors and constraints under which the popular music industry functions and thus make a contribution to our understanding of this most important cultural industry.

Chapter 2 starts us off by examining the role of the music industry within the expanding global entertainment industry and introducing some key concepts. In Chapter 3 we will locate the study of popular music within theoretical approaches to the concepts of mass culture and popular culture. The chapter then moves on to a more specific examination of definitions of popular music and ends by relating the study of popular music to mass communication research. Chapter 4 is a description of the developments taking place in the popular music industry. The main actors in the music industry are also introduced.

Chapter 5 introduces the production of culture model. Here it will be suggested that the subsystems of production and consumption of culture are analytically and factually distinct and that the relationships within the sectors of production and consumption, respectively, are much stronger than the connections between them. Chapter 6 examines the consumption system of popular music and takes up the role of technology. Chapter 7 is devoted to the largest and single most important market for commercial music, the United States. Chapter 8 looks at the music industry changes taking place in a small country, Sweden. Chapter 9 is the final chapter which draws together and summarizes the key findings of the different aspects of the study. Implications of recent trends will be discussed along with suggestions as to where the music business is headed.

Before we start, American media scholar Ben Bagdikian gives us a timely reminder that there is a dark side to McLuhan's vision of a 'global village' in an era when: 'one medium can be used to promote the same idea, product, celebrity, or politician in another medium, both owned by the same corporation. Each of the new global giants aims for control of as many different media as possible: news, magazines, radio, television, books, motion pictures, cable systems, satellite channels, recordings, video-cassettes, and ownership of movie houses' (Bagdikian, 1990: 243). Let us now begin our journey by looking a little closer at these 'global giants'.

Chapter 2

Music and the entertainment industry

The world is our audience.
                (Time Warner)

Think globally – act locally.
                (Sony)

A truly global organization.
                (Thorn–EMI)

A European based global recording company.
                (Polygram)

Globalize local repertoire.
                (BMG)

In recent years the international music companies have begun to stress that they are global organizations. Globalization in their case, and as reflected in company annual reports, means the organization of production, distribution and consumption of cultural goods on a world scale market. The flow of information, ideas and cultural artifacts on a global scale has greatly increased in recent decades, due in part to the many developments of new communication technology. Appadurai (1990: 296) suggests five dimensions of cultural flow: ethnoscapes, technoscapes, finanscapes, mediascapes and ideoscapes, which are all interconnected. Ethnoscapes are made up of the landscapes of people representing the world we inhabit. Amongst these we find tourists, immigrants, refugees, and other groups of migrant people who are on the move. Technoscapes refer to the global arrangement and rapid movement of technology. Finanscapes consist of the disposition and transfer of global economic capital. The fourth dimension of global cultural flow, mediascapes, describes both the distribution of information technology and the images of the world that the media create. The final dimension, ideoscapes, are linked to the building of politically or ideologically defined images. In simplified terms, Appadurai's five dimensions apply to the global flow of people, machinery, money, images and ideas.

According to Appadurai, it is no longer fruitful to try to understand the new global cultural economy by using old models of conflict that contrast the centre versus the periphery. In most of these models of 'cultural imperialism' an underlying concern or fear of 'cultural homogenization' and/or 'cultural synchronization' (Hamelink, 1983; Schiller, 1976) is expressed in the wake of growing Americanization and commodification. What is clear is that in the 1990s the international media environment is far more complex than that suggested by earlier models of media imperialism.

Keeping these reflections in sight, the study of transnational music production should be able to tell us something about the ways in which international capital works in the field of popular culture and specifically the entertainment industry. For example, a question that is currently in vogue is: Are we experiencing the rise of a global homogenous world culture, and if so, will this process still allow for smaller heterogeneous local cultural traditions? Appadurai (1990: 295) claims, for example, that 'the central problem of today's global interactions is the tension between cultural homogenization and cultural heterogenization'. This observation gives us cause for reflection as we now turn our attention to the role of popular music in the entertainment industry.

THE GLOBAL ENTERTAINMENT INDUSTRY

Contemporary entertainment is almost always big business in western societies and is almost always related in one way or another to the mass media and the mass communication process. Turow (1992a: 9) defines mass media as the 'technological vehicles through which mass communication takes place'. Mass communication is often defined as the industrialized production, reproduction and multiple distribution of messages through technological devices. Entertain, if we look in the dictionary, means to 'divert attention' or to 'keep steady, busy, or amused'. The entertainment industry then, by definition, 'involves the interorganizational creation and release of performances (narrative or nonnarrative, recorded or live) to attract audiences for financial profit rather than for explicitly educational, journalistic, political or advertising goals' (Turow, 1991: 166).

Given this definition, it is important to understand that the entertainment industry generates billions of dollars a year in revenues worldwide and is rapidly growing. Every year consumers around the world buy $300 billion worth of movie tickets, compact discs, videotapes and other entertainment products. Video and computer games now account for the greatest revenues worldwide, followed thereafter by television, sound recordings (phonograms), books and magazines, and then films (Bernstein, 1990).

At the same time, as noted above, it is really no longer fruitful to talk about American 'cultural imperialism' at the level of ownership in the entertainment industry. European and Japanese companies have proved to be at least as imperialistic as their American counterparts. It makes more sense to discuss the few 'transnational' companies that dominate today's world market. The transnationals certainly see themselves as players on a world scale. Advances in communications technology have weakened the nature of traditional national boundaries. One can talk about an increasing concentration of media ownership combined with a globalization of the market.

It used to be the case that Hollywood film, television and record producers saw foreign distribution as a lucrative byproduct, money to be made after earning back costs and hopefully turning a profit in the domestic American market. In recent years it is increasingly the case that producers, distributors and investors target the international market from the very beginning of every new project. Still, it is important to remember that much of the information and entertainment material owned by non-American companies is still created by Americans, for the simple reason that Los Angeles remains the film, music and television production capital of the global entertainment industry.

The entertainment industry thrives on producing global stars to expose across a wide range of media: film, music, videos, television, books, magazines and advertising included. The music industry is obviously an important link in this process as nothing crosses borders and cultural boundaries easier than music. In fact, one could argue quite persuasively that music is perhaps the essential component in linking the different sectors of the global entertainment industry. The entertainment industry has undergone tremendous changes in at least three readily defined areas: integration, concentration and internationalization. These phenomena are interrelated as will be seen below.

INTERNATIONALIZATION

The ownership of major entertainment enterprises has become increasingly internationalized, reflecting the economic interdependence among nations which Porter (1980) has repeatedly observed. In the entertainment industries it goes beyond internationalization of ownership. American film, television, video, record and music publishing companies now derive at least 50 per cent of their revenues from foreign markets, and must therefore consider the tastes of consumers in other countries as well as those of American consumers. One of the reasons why film producers pay million dollar fees to movie stars such as Sylvester Stallone, Arnold Schwarzenegger, Mel Gibson and Bruce Willis, is the simple fact that in the right sort of film with lots of action and little dialogue, enormous box office returns can be derived outside the United States. Escalating film production costs have made thinking about the foreign market crucial. The same logic is at work in the music industry for superstars such as Madonna and Michael Jackson.

In December 1993, President Clinton hailed the 'breakthrough' in the global trade negotiations and declared, 'We are now on the verge of an historic victory to open foreign markets to American products' (*New York Times*, 14 Dec. 1993). The American president made the remarks at the conclusion of the General Agreement on Tariffs and Trade (GATT) negotiations held in Geneva. One major arena of contention was the US insistence that European countries open their markets to an unrestrained flow of American movies, videos and music. The American Trade Representative and the European Community's Trade Commissioner 'agreed to disagree', with the Europeans rejecting a complete opening of their movie, music and other entertainment sectors. Washington thus chose not to sign the audiovisual section of the global trade liberalization package known as the Uruguay Round. The EC insisted that the entertainment sector in its member countries be at least 50 per cent of European origin whenever practicable and allows its movie sector to enjoy subsidies. The American negotiator stated that the United States was unable to accept that people can be controlled in what they want to see and hear.

Jack Valenti, head of the Motion Picture Export Association of America, made the American position on European imposed restrictions very clear. Those in the European Community who were imposing trade restrictions on American media products were using the excuse of protecting 'national cultures' as a way to increase their own companies' revenue at the expense of American companies. Valenti also described the American entertainment industry as one of the country's 'glittering trade jewels', with a surplus of over $3 billion annually in balance of trade (Gelman, 1990: 12).

The vertical and horizontal integration of the music, film and television production and publishing industries, an alignment of technology development and ownership that is coupled to production and distribution control, has never been more closely linked to the power centres of the media and electronics industries in America, Europe and Japan. It will be interesting to see if rather than hobble American popular culture export, the foreign ownership of once American entertainment companies, in the long run, increases its exposure around the world.

INTEGRATION AND CONCENTRATION

The international 'flow' of communication is a complex phenomenon which has been analysed from different perspectives, using different types of evidence. Cultural imperialism, cultural domination, cultural dependency and media imperialism are concepts that have been used (often ambiguously) by social scientists and laypeople alike. These terms are either used to express a general dissatisfaction with a supposed 'one way' flow of culture and information or as a basic concept for the systematic analysis of media flows and structures.

Numerous scholars (Hamelink, 1983; Schiller, 1984; Smythe, 1981) have claimed that transnational corporations and the internationalization of capital are the dominant central features of the present world order. The United Nations (Guback and Varis, 1982) has defined transnational corporations according to four main criteria: size, oligarchic nature, a large number of foreign subsidiaries and branch offices, and origins in the developed countries.

In addition to transnational corporations, the terms multinational, international and global corporations are often used. Multinational implies however that the economic interests of several countries are involved as equal partners, which is rarely the case. The word international also implies some sort of equal principles based on internationalism, which is equally rare. Globalization generally refers to the organization of production, distribution and consumption of cultural goods on a world-scale market. The global aspect, for its part, usually refers to the geographic scope of operations. Following the UN example we will use the term transnational corporations (TNC) which is viewed as the best description of the activities and characteristics of these corporations.

The historical development of the commercial media in most western countries can be divided into two principal periods. The first phase is one of industrialization, characterized by the emergence of distinct processes of production and distribution. This involves the commercial and technological development of a production process, increasingly geared to deal with, and expand, mass consumption and demand. Media markets at this stage tend to be 'supply limited', meaning that as many books, newspapers and records and so on that can be produced can and will be absorbed within the growing contours of demand. They also tend to be supplied by a large number of relatively small-scale competing organizations (Hamelink, 1983).

The second phase of development is one of concentration: media markets become saturated and contract, competition fluctuates and tensions develop between production and consumption. In this stage media industries provide clear examples of the monopolistic tendencies of capitalistic economies, whereby market sectors become dominated by a decreasing number of large-scale companies.

Some spectacular mergers and takeovers amongst media companies have allowed the rapid growth of the contemporary media conglomerates. These shifts of capital have aroused concern in some circles and led to debate about the control of the media. Most debaters agree that the media are the base of a culture industry that requires special treatment by the public authorities. There is general concern that levels of ownership and market concentration that would be tolerable in other economic fields may be undesirable in the media industry. Those against media concentration stress the value of cultural aspects over market economics. The opposing new liberal argument claims that the market assigns the resources and regulates the economy more efficiently than the state. The ownership of the media and the role the media should play in society are the topics of much debate within the European Union and will continue to be so for some time.

According to Sánchez-Tabernero (1993: 7), concentration in a media market can be defined as 'an increase in the presence of one or a handful of media companies in any market as a result of various possible processes: acquisitions, mergers, deals with other companies, or even the disappearance of competitors'. Concentration is a measure of the degree to which the largest companies control production, employment, or other indicators of size in an industry in a market. Concentration is measured by observing within specified markets the ratio of total sales of the top companies to the total sales of the industry as a whole. Traditional thresholds for concern that concentration is leading to oligopolistic or monopolistic activities that will have an adverse effect on the marketplace have been when the top four firms control more than 50 per cent of a market or the top eight firms more than 70 per cent.

There are generally two measurements used in discussing levels of concentration. Concentration of ownership considers the amount of an industry controlled by individual firms. This is the usual presentation of absolute numbers: profits, ranking according to total turnover and the number of employees in the media company. Secondly there is concentration of the market which is the presentation of actual market shares of the main media companies in a given market. This concentration of media production is according to Hamelink (1983) the result of three inter-linked economic processes: integration, diversification and internationalization. Four types of integration can be identified which correspond to the different processes of growth of media companies: vertical, horizontal, international and multimedia.

Vertical integration refers to situations where a company either partly or completely controls the channels of production and distribution of a particular media market. The vertical integration strategy implies that a company should be in a dominant position in a variety of different, though connected, businesses. There are two types of vertical integration to be found: upstream and downstream. Upstream vertical integration implies broadcasters moving into production, developing their own skills and buying library programmes; hardware manufacturers moving into production, mainly through acquisitions; and distributors buying into production. Downstream vertical integration refers to producers moving into broadcasting through mergers and acquisitions; and broadcasters moving into distribution. In recent years the media conglomerates have been looking for programming acquisitions. This upstream vertical intregration has been recently demonstrated by Matsushita's acquisition of MCA/Universal, as well as Sony's purchase of Columbia Pictures/CBS Records, and News Corporation's acquisition of 20th Century Fox.

Companies are looking for the control of both the revenues and cultural products which explains why production is the most common objective of 'upstream' integration. The new entrants are seeking synergy with their existing business. The appearance of global audiovisual groups is generating a higher level of vertical integration. Japanese companies like Sony and Matsushita, which have hardware expertise, try to avoid dependency upon American programmes by purchasing the company source. Likewise European companies have been acquiring American software capabilities while American companies have been exporting their programmes and products as well as their knowhow concerning cable television. This triad between America, Europe and Japan is depicted in Figure 2.1.

Horizontal integration implies a policy of growth which goes beyond the idea of controlling the channels of production and distribution of a specific media industry. Horizontal integration exists when a company owns the same type of media in different markets: newspapers, radio stations, television stations, etc. This strategy allows a high level of

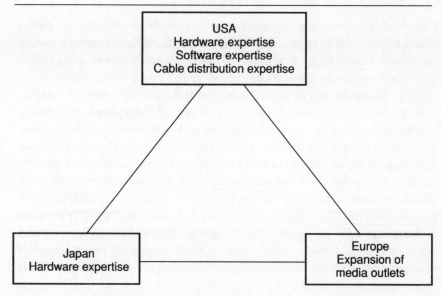

Figure 2.1 Triad: USA, Japan, Europe

specialization to be attained; the media companies enter into various new markets, with a product which they have successfully managed in its original market.

In the majority of cases, companies involved in horizontal integration tend to undertake other types of integration: vertical, multimedia or both at the same time. The link between horizontal and multimedia integration is explained by their similar criteria for growth; in the first instance, the companies export successful products to new markets; in the second, they introduce new products into markets in which they are already present.

Multimedia integration thus refers to the control of various media by one company. The diversification of newspaper publishing towards book or magazine industries is often stated as an example. However, full multimedia integration requires cross-ownership between the printed and audiovisual media (newspapers and television). Multimedia integration in the field of electronic and audiovisual media (radio, television, cable, satellite, film) is more common (see Sánchez-Tabernero, 1993). This 'real' multimedia integration occurred during the 1980s when the audiovisual media were deregulated and cross-ownership became possible in many countries.

The integration of music organizations has been mostly horizontal and vertical. Horizontal integration occurs when one company takes over or buys into the operations of others in the same sector. So, for our music example, this refers to the buying up of small and medium-size record companies by the larger firms. The production and distribution of phonograms has rapidly become concentrated in the hands of a small number of large transnationals with increasing control over their market sector.

Vertical integration describes the process whereby music companies extend their operations to encompass the final distribution of the finished product, or to acquire control of the initial stages of manufacture and basic raw material extraction and processing. For our music example this includes the merging of distinct stages in the path of a phonogram from idea to consumption, including production, distribution and retailing. The phonogram company buys up the existing recording studios, CD pressing and cassette copying plants, printing works, distribution companies and retail outlets. In both horizontal and vertical integration the commercial control over existing and emerging technologies of production and consumption is vital.

Diversification is another yet broader economic strategy whereby media companies extend and spread their commercial interests and hence their potential for profitability across other sectors of industrial production. Faced with declining markets and decreasing profitability, media companies often attempt to distribute their investments across a wide range of operations. These diversified interests may extend across the general sectors of the leisure and entertainment industries resulting in communication conglomerates such as, in our case, Time Warner, Thorn–EMI, Sony, BMG, MCA and Polygram.

The highly concentrated structure of different media sectors is once again best illustrated by the concentration ratio, which expresses the proportion of each market sector owned and controlled by the leading firms. This has revealed that competition within media sectors is increasingly controlled by a declining number of large-scale corporations. At the same time, there has been a shift towards combining different sectors of media production and output, often with the result that multimedia conglomerates accumulate and extend their control in several sectors simultaneously.

One of the major driving forces involved in the process of concentration is the desire to maintain or increase the control over the market in both its present formation as well as to be prepared to exploit its future possibilities. The diversification of interests across a broad range of media not only enables companies to spread their risks and to cushion their investments against periods of economic recession. It can also facilitate highly profitable production strategies in that an organization that controls, or has access to, a range of different types of media and forms of cultural production and distribution, can cross markets or at least negotiate a portion of a single media product. For example, both films and music have profitable 'spin off' potential in other areas. Clearly, under certain conditions it pays to expand the market in this way, to produce and expand consumption across sectors. Audiences who have seen the film, may buy the book, the magazine with the star on the cover, the music from the soundtrack and maybe a T shirt. They may even rent the video or watch the film again on television or listen to the theme song on radio or music television.

It is important at this point to note that the international activity of the major phonogram companies is partly determined by their interaction with other international organs such as the international copyright organizations. The recording industry has its own international lobby organization, the International Federation of Phonogram and Videogram Producers (IFPI), which is active in intergovernmental debates regarding the protection of the rights of composers, recording artists and producers. The primary aim of the IFPI is to encourage governments to adhere to the existing international copyright conventions which will enable the industry to increase its earnings from the secondary usage of recorded music such as from songs played on the radio or television.

On the national level, government policy can often affect the activities of transnationals in specific countries. Some countries, for example, will not allow the transnationals to set up branch plants or subsidiaries. National governments, as in Canada, can even set quotas limiting the amount of foreign recorded music on national or local broadcast media. National musicians' unions can prohibit the use of backing tracks or 'play back' performances when artists appear on television to promote their songs.

On the local level are the audiences or music consumers, the music makers, as well as the local music enthusiasts, who, in growing numbers, utilize inexpensive musical industry technology to start their own local recording studios and modest phonogram productions. The role of the transnationals at the local level is double edged: on the one hand to sell their recordings of a few international stars, while at the same time identifying new trends, new artists and new sounds to exploit internationally. The different processes that occur both within and between these levels are vital to understanding how the phonogram industry works.

In this study we will not only distinguish between the international, national and local levels but also between centralized (closed) and decentralized (open) levels of production. We will use the terminology employed in world systems analysis (Wallerstein, 1975; Hopkins and Wallerstein,

1982). 'Core' is used for centralized production (usually international but sometimes national as opposed to local, especially in the United States and the UK) and 'peripheral' for decentralized production (usually to designate the combination of national and local as distinct from the international level). 'Regional' is sometimes used to apply to areas including several countries such as Scandinavia.

SOME OF THE PLAYERS

The trend towards concentration that characterized the takeover and fusion binge of the 1980s was also felt throughout the entire entertainment industry and especially the music industry. The Big Six major phonogram companies – Sony, Warner, Polygram, EMI, BMG and MCA – now account for over 90 per cent of US sales and an estimated 70 to 80 per cent of worldwide sales.

Japanese electronics giant Sony purchased CBS Records for $2.2 billion and then purchased Columbia Pictures for $3.4 billion. Time/Life's 1990 merger with Warner Communications created Time Warner, the world's largest communications company and significantly, the only American enterprise of that magnitude in a world dominated by multinational communications conglomerates such as Bertelsmann (Germany), Hachette (France) and Murdoch's News Corporation. Polygram Records, itself a subsidiary of The Netherlands multinational electronics giant Philips, acquired both Island Records and A&M Records. British EMI, a division of multinational Thorn, acquired independent music publishers SBK as well as Chrysalis Records and Virgin Records. The German BMG, a division of media giant Bertelsmann, purchased both RCA Records and Arista Records. And last but not least, in 1990 Matsushita Electric Industrial, which is twice the size of Sony, purchased MCA, parent of Universal Pictures and MCA records.

It is not only the music industry which is dominated by a few firms. In the United States, the motion picture industry today is ruled by seven major film studios that engage in the financing, production and distribution of films: Universal Pictures (a division of MCA which was acquired by Matsushita Electrical Industrial in December 1990), Columbia Pictures (acquired by Sony in 1989), 20th Century Fox (now a subsidiary of Rupert Murdoch's News Corporation), MGM/UA (acquired by Pathé and presently controlled by Credit Lyonnais Netherlands), Warner Brothers (a subsidiary of Time Warner), Paramount Pictures (a subsidiary of Paramount Communications) and The Walt Disney Company (Buena Vista). Together with Orion and TriStar, the major film companies control

Table 2.1 Media corporations after total revenues, 1992

1	Time Warner (USA)
2	Bertelsmann (Germany)
3	Capital Cities/ABC (USA)
4	News Corporation (Australia/UK/USA)
5	Hachette (France)
6	RCA/NBC (USA)
7	Gannett Company (USA)
8	Gulf and Western (USA)
9	Finninvest (Italy)
10	CBS (USA)

Source: Company reports

the distribution of American motion pictures in the United States as well as throughout the rest of the world. The high cost of distributing movies to the mainstream market means that independent production companies must try to convince one of the majors to carry their output if they are to have a chance of reaching a large public.

Even though the size of the major music and film companies is quite impressive in their own right they are often buried away within much larger media and electronics conglomerates and usually only account for between 5 and 25 per cent of total company revenues. If we take for example the electronics industry who manufacture the *hardware* for the entertainment industry we find that General Electric, Matsushita, Philips, Sony and Siemens are the largest companies in terms of revenues. If we look to the media corporations who produce the *software* we find in terms of total revenues the largest ranking companies are Time Warner, Bertelsmann, Capital Cities/ABC, News Corporation and Hachette.

If we rank order the largest transnational media corporations according to worldwide revenues as reported in company annual reports we come up with the list shown in Table 2.1.

Let's look a little closer at some of the companies in the media hardware and software industries. The *Sony* Corporation is the Japanese parent company that is currently divided into the Sony Electronics Corporation and the Sony Software Corporation. The Sony Electronics Corporation is responsible for the *hardware*, that is, the electronics, recording, manufacturing and marketing operations. The Sony Software Corporation consists of three different divisions: Sony Music Entertainment, Sony Pictures Entertainment and Sony Electronic Publishing. As the name implies these corporate divisions are in the business of producing *software*.

Sony had $26 billion in sales in 1991. It reigns unchallenged as the most consistently inventive consumer electronics enterprise in the world. Sony popularized the pocket size transistor radio, the battery-powered TV set, the VCR, the camcorder and the walkman portable cassette player. Worldwide Sony employs 112,900 people. In 1991 the company spent $1.5 billion supporting their research and product development (R&D) efforts – roughly 5.7 per cent of revenues. Sony founder, Masaru Ibuka, explains: 'The key to success for Sony, and to everything in business, science, and technology for that matter, is never to follow the others' (Schlender, 1992: 23). Similarly, current chairman, Akio Morita, states: 'Our basic concept has always been this – to give new convenience, or new methods, or new benefits, to the general public with our technology' (ibid.: 23).

Sony is trying for the edge in the digital future, by selling the latest machines as well as the software they use. The digital future is simply 'computing plus entertainment', says Michael Schulhof, vice-chairman of Sony America. So the key software is movies and music, which is one reason Sony bought Columbia Pictures and CBS Records. 'I spent $8 billion of Sony's money developing this strategy', says Schulhof. 'We're the best positioned company in the world' (Neff, 1992: 96). Indeed, perhaps only rival Matsushita, owner of MCA, comes close to matching Sony's mix of digital hardware and entertainment software. It is supposed to all come together in a series of products on CD-ROM for storing images digitally with full colour, motion and sound. 'Our new CD medium will be used for everything: entertainment, computing, data storage, and telecommunications', says Mr Idei of Sony (ibid.: 97). Sony is focusing on what another executive calls the 'three Ps' of the digital revolution: personal entertainment, personal information and personal communications. The same source noted that, 'the lines between hardware and software are getting fuzzier all the time'. Sony appears to have made a strategic commitment to full integration of electronics and entertainment.

The Japanese *Matsushita* corporation is the world's largest consumer electronics firm with 1990 revenues of $38 billion. Matsushita produces the JVC line of consumer electronics. Matsushita bought the MCA entertainment company and Universal Pictures for $6.1 billion in 1990. The same year the company spent $3 billion on research and development or 6.2 per cent of total sales. For an electronic hardware firm like Matsushita the MCA purchase is a way of ensuring an immensely valuable supply of software: the movies, CDs and films that can be played on the machines Matsushita sells. Matsushita hopes to put half a century's worth of MCA creative output into new CDs, videotapes, laser discs and new formats.

The American *Time Warner* organization claims to be the largest media company in the world. The Time Warner organization includes the Time-Life book and magazine publishers (*Time*, *Life*, *Fortune*, *Sports Illustrated*), Warner Brothers film studio, Lorimar Telepictures (world's largest TV production company), Warner Music company, DC Comics, and the Home Box Office cable TV channel. Time Warner's total revenue for 1991 amounted to $12 billion. This total was divided into: film 25 per cent, music 24 per cent, magazines and books 24 per cent, cable TV systems 16 per cent and television production 11 per cent.

The German *Bertelsmann* company has 44,000 employees in 30 countries around the world. Bertelsmann controls the RTL-Plus and Première TV channels in Europe. The publishing (books, magazines, newspapers) and recording industries are its principal activities in the global marketplace. The Bertelsmann group has positioned itself well in the entertainment software business in the belief that this is where future profits are to be made. Consequently, a BMG executive expressed the international strategy; 'while increasing in complexity and becoming even more fiercely competitive, this sector of the economy will continue to grow. Success will depend on skill, experience and creativity in each market segment and – to the extent that entertainment properties of international importance are involved – a global infrastructure'.

News Corporation is the company controlled by Rupert Murdoch (now an American citizen). News Corporation controls or owns the *Sun*, *News of the World* and the *Sunday Times* newspapers among others, as well as the TV Guide magazines. News Corporation also owns the US Fox TV network, 20th Century Fox film studios, Harper & Row Books and is part owner of Reuters news bureau. They also control the Sky satellite TV channel. News Corporation's total revenue for 1991 amounted to $8.6 billion. This was broken down as follows: Newspapers 39 per cent, films 20 per cent, book publishing 14 per cent, television 12 per cent, magazines 12 per cent and commercial printing 5 per cent.

SYNERGY

One can identify numerous advantages for media companies that increased concentration may provide. These include: power and prestige for owners and managers; influence over public opinion; synergies between various media of each company; dominance of markets; sharing of skills between companies merged or acquired; economies of scale; diversification of risks; major possibilities for innovation; and career opportunities for employees.

In the 1990s, *synergy* has been the preferred topic of conversation amongst entertainment industry executives. Here we refer to the economic gain caused by the ownership or control of various media by one media company. Synergy means the coordination of parts of a company so that the whole actually turns out to be worth more than the sum of its parts acting alone, without helping one another. Sánchez-Tabernero (1993: 163) explains that:

> the synergetic effect means that the profit of a company increases as a result of certain 'benefits' or advantages resulting from the simultaneous ownership of various media. Managers may find that certain launches of 'products' or acquisitions are more successful and profitable; moreover, they may achieve certain synergies in terms of advertising, distribution, financing, cross promotion and management, and may therefore increase the profitability of each separate medium.

Accordingly one Time Warner executive viewed his vision of the future as follows:

> A media company that intended to compete successfully in this environment would have to be heard and big enough to hold consumer attention. It would have to propose products and synergies that only a large, versatile organization could offer. It'd have to be able to move its products throughout the emerging global marketplace and amortize its costs over as many distribution networks as possible ... Long-term, we saw the world accommodating perhaps a half-dozen global media companies, and we intended to be one of them ... What we wanted was solid vertical integration so we could offer synergies that would bring together magazines, publishing ventures, studios, cable channels, and other activities into a coherent operation.
>
> (quoted in Turow, 1992b: 688)

What this means is that the large media corporations have gathered under their corporate umbrellas different firms that represent production and distribution interests in a variety of media. As audiences become fragmented (i.e. smaller) the idea is to move the creative material across as many outlets as possible to justify production. This means interconnecting interests, personnel, products and services of many parts of their conglomerates so as to cover all opportunities as efficiently as possible. Turow (1991: 172) notes that to do this they 'view the various companies of a media conglomerate as parts of a unified whole that should work together to move products across new and old media' (synergy); and by trying to 'exploit its strengths across media by forging joint licensing, syndication, and public relations ventures with other established companies'. Turow (1991) points out that this increasing dependency on media 'tie ins' is making the entertainment industry look more and more like the Disney corporation which has always promoted a 'total package' when releasing new movies. Hence we have witnessed the tremendous growth of the 'blockbuster' where a book becomes a movie with the obligatory sound-track album featuring music videos by major artists where glimpses of the film are prominently exposed (Whitney Houston's song and video, 'I Will Always Love You', from the soundtrack album of the movie, *The Bodyguard*, is a prime example).

Synergy is not without its problems and is not always as easy to imple-ment in practice as it is in theory. In an era of mergers and fusion it is not always easy for people coming from different companies with different company cultures to plan and work jointly on projects. Chains of decision making are not easily broken, especially if the projected goal is clothed in somewhat abstract notions such as 'increased cross-media activity'. Time Warner, the world's largest media conglomerate, is a good example. Time Warner had a debt of $8.7 billion at the end of 1991 and has profited very little from attempts at synergy, perhaps because each medium and market has its own unique circumstances.

Consequently, Time Warner and the other media conglomerates are involved in a series of 'non-competitive strategic alliances'. These 'joint ventures' are at least partly motivated as a way of sharing the investment and the risk entailed in the development of new products and markets. A Bertelsmann executive stressed that, 'the creation of joint-ventures is unquestionably one of the more interesting prospects of the 1990s'.

ARTISTS AND MEGADEALS

The move into the 'information age' was supposed to be accompanied by a 'leisure time revolution' according to which people would have far more time for leisure. Whether this has actually happened or not we can leave to others to judge. It is certainly true that with the onslaught of new tech-nologies and entertainment industry products to choose amongst, it has become increasingly more difficult to capture the attention of the public. This difficulty has in turn led to an increase in expenditures for familiar, tried and tested talent. The transnational music industry has found that its average investment in a recording by a new and non-established artist (including artist advance, recording costs, manufacturing and distribution costs and costs for advertising and promotion) can approach half a million dollars, while its investment in a recording by a major artist can escalate

Table 2.2 Superstar size contracts

	$	
Michael Jackson	65m	Sony
Madonna	60m	Time Warner
Rolling Stones	44m	EMI–Virgin
Aerosmith	37m	Sony
Janet Jackson	32m	EMI–Virgin
Motley Crüe	25m	Time Warner

Source: Company reports and music trade press

into several million dollars. This is in an industry where only two out of ten releases generate enough income to cover their own costs. Given the current economic climate it is not surprising that record company executives have more often than not in recent years elected to spend the big money on promoting the big stars.

The sale of so many record labels for so much money has also made the recording artists realize that they are a large part of the overall value of the record companies – something that hasn't been taken into account in previous contract negotiations. In recent years more and more superstar artists have become free agents after fulfilling their contracts. Michael Jackson, Janet Jackson, Madonna, Aerosmith, Paul McCartney, the Rolling Stones, Elton John, Paul Simon, REM and Bob Dylan all opted to test their own value on the open market rather than renegotiate contracts, and subsequently struck major deals. The size of some of the deals in US dollars are as shown in Table 2.2 as reported in the music trade press.

As Goodman has noted: 'Superstars like Madonna or Michael Jackson are starting to recognize that they are a keystone in a global business that didn't exist when they first signed their contracts. So now it's not just about music or even the number of records or concert tickets you can sell, but about fame and who has the highest profile to offer an international media giant struggling to put a human face on its far flung operations' (Goodman, 1992: 51). As an entertainment industry lawyer explained: 'these stars aren't just selling in the US – they're being marketed on a global level, because they have global appeal'.

Traditionally, recording contracts pay the artist a set amount of the sale price of a recording. Before working on an album, the artist receives an advance against future royalties. The bigger the artist, the bigger the royalty and the bigger the advance. Aerosmith's four-album deal with

Sony Music reportedly includes $13.5 million in advances, $6 million for new product and an additional $7.5 million for the continued use of their back catalogue. The group's royalty rate is approximately 25 per cent of each recording's wholesale price, one of the highest in the business. They are also to receive a $5 million royalty advance on each album.

Michael Jackson's contract has a profit-sharing feature that is unique to the industry but could be a sign of things to come. Jackson and Sony have in essence become partners. Jackson now gets less money upfront. He used to receive an $18 million advance on every album, he now gets $5 million. His royalty rate is one of the best in the business at 25 per cent of the wholesale price. In return for taking less money as an advance, he now gets a piece of the profits beyond his royalty. Jackson now receives half of the profits that normally go to the record company. In addition, Sony has provided Jackson with his own record label, Nation, for producing other artists, and a film production deal with Sony's Columbia Pictures. In order for the deal to have maximum effect, Jackson must remain one of the world's best selling artists for some time to come. Given the mutually beneficial nature of the deal both Jackson and Sony have a vital interest to protect. One can only speculate on whether Jackson's trouble with the law and marriage to Lisa Marie Presley will hurt or help his music career.

Madonna signed a $60 million multimedia deal with Time Warner. Included were a seven-year deal for her own record company, HBO specials, videos, films, books, merchandise and six albums. Time Warner will pay Madonna a $5 million advance for each album, put up $2 million for two HBO specials, and spend $5 million a year to underwrite Madonna's new record label (Tsiantar and Hammer, 1992: 45). Madonna's albums have sold an average of 9 million copies each worldwide, so theoretically both artist and company will profit from the deal. In fact, Time Warner usually feature Madonna's picture prominently in its annual report. Madonna in turn has made herself one of the most recognized people in the world and probably Time Warner's most effective corporate symbol after Bugs Bunny!

Somehow Madonna manages to survive all the negative publicity generated around her career. In 1989, a Pepsi-Cola television commercial starring Madonna provoked a number of religious organizations to anger. The spot showed Madonna performing her song, 'Like a Prayer'. The religious organizations contended that the music video from which the spot was made was blasphemous. They pointed to the singer's sexual posturing while surrounded by religious symbols such as a crucifix. They insisted that the commercial be withdrawn and it was. The song and album went on to be a giant hit. Madonna has also constantly received bad press from her attempts at acting and her book, *Sex*, was generally panned. Still Madonna survives, giving support to the old maxim that 'bad publicity is better than no publicity'.

Long-term contracts with star artists have traditionally been the key for the record companies. Most labels still guarantee just one or two albums, while insisting on options for several more should the artist succeed. The phonogram industry also has a need for product innovation. Innovation means changing something that exists, creating something new. There is a constant search for new sounds, new artists and hopefully the 'next big thing'.

As Tremlett has pointed out:

> The search for new product is more competitive. The stakes are high with record companies reluctant to invest in new artists when there are so many in the market-place. And now, with the expanded world market, the rewards are so great that even minor artists expect to spend a year or more promoting new product. The principles have stayed the same, but the pace has changed. The Beatles released seven albums in just over three years. Now, top product has a long life, with the artists packaged more neatly.
>
> (Tremlett, 1990: 186)

As a case in point, Michael Jackson worked *Thriller* for five years before releasing his next LP, *Bad*, and then waited another four years before releasing *Dangerous* in 1991.

It also may no longer be any use turning to the best seller charts for confirmation of an artist's status. Chart success and financial success are not necessarily synonymous. Established artists like the Rolling Stones or Bruce Springsteen have not had many hit singles for years but the truth of the matter is that they no longer need to worry about chart success. Each has a firm fan base, a constant demand for concert tours, steady album sales, and, most of all, royalty income flowing in from around the world.

In 1992 and 1993 ageing artists such as Eric Clapton, Rod Stewart, and Neil Young were estimated to have sold more albums than at any other time in their long careers. This was partially due to their respective MTV *Unplugged* appearances which apparently won them a new, younger audience. This new audience also bought their old albums. Back catalogue is generally cited these days as accounting for about 40 per cent of all sales. An even more fascinating, if not somewhat macabre situation is revealed in the 1992 sales statistics for dead artists as shown in Table 2.3.

Table 2.3 Dead gold: album sales by dead artists in the USA, 1992

Elvis Presley	1,500,000
The Doors	1,000,000
Jimi Hendrix	900,000
Bob Marley	550,000
Roy Orbison	500,000
Janis Joplin	400,000

Source: Record company estimates

Not surprisingly, Elvis leads the dead gold miners with sales of over one and a half million albums sold. More than one comedian has noted that death is often a 'good career move'.

TROUBLE AHEAD

In 1993 George Michael (aka Giorgios Panayiotou) filed a suit claiming his long-term recording contract with Sony Music Entertainment amounted to an unreasonable restraint of trade. Fighting what could turn out to be a landmark case against the international recording industry, Michael wants to declare his contract null and void. At stake, if Michael wins, is that free agency could be introduced into the music business. This would make it easier for artists to follow their creative and financial inclinations, and effectivly label-hop with greater frequency. This would significantly weaken the ability of record companies to control the product market and to build up artist catalogues that help to maintain a stable production process.

The suit complains that under Michael's eight-album, fifteen-year deal, Sony not only lacks any obligation to release recordings it concludes are artistically or commercially unacceptable, it can also stop him from recording for anyone else. Michael's lawyer claimed, 'Recording is the lynchpin of all his professional activities. Without recording he seriously underachieves or fades entirely from the scene' (Soocher, 1993: 34). Sony has countered by arguing that the contract is morally and legally binding and mutually fruitful. Despite Sony's advance to Michael of $19.4 million in 1988, lawyers argued the case was not about money but about a contract that bound Michael to the company on terms capable of being worked to his disadvantage.

Sony says it needs lengthy contracts with recording artists to invest in the promotion of new stars while Michael has said the contract inhibits his professional career and Sony treats him as 'little more than software'.

Michael claims the six companies that dominate the worldwide industry – Sony, EMI, Warner, BMG, Polygram and MCA – offer standard contracts that are often loaded in favour of the company. 'Musicians do not come in regimented shapes and sizes, but are individuals who change and evolve together with their audiences', Michael has said. 'Sony obviously views this as a great inconvenience. They have developed hard sell, high profile sales techniques, and their stance is that if George Michael, or any other artist for that matter, does not wish to conform to Sony's current ideas, there are plenty of hungry young acts who will.' Sony has countered by saying, 'We are saddened and surprised by the action George has taken against Sony Music. There is a serious moral as well as legal commitment attached to any contract and we will not only honor it, but vigorously defend it' (Shadbolt, 1993: 1).

At the time of writing, Sony had won the first round but Michael has appealed against the decision. The latest superstar to challenge the transnationals is the Symbol, formerly known as Prince. The Symbol wants out of his recording contract with Warner Music and has recently been seen performing live and on video with the word 'slave' written on his face, slave referring to the Symbol's position in his relationship to his master, Warner Music.

This all sounds very close to the description rendered by Tremlett: 'The music industry is nothing more than that: an industry that makes money out of music, dealing and trading in this commodity with as much refinement as the second-hand car trade' (1990: 175). Depending on the outcome of these litigation processes the relationship between artist and company might well never be the same again, thus having tremendous consequences for the future of the entire music industry.

Chapter 3

Music as popular culture

Rock 'n' roll is the most brutal, ugly, desperate, vicious form of expression it has been my misfortune to hear.

(Frank Sinatra, testifying before the US
Congress Payola hearings in 1958)

Music can and has been described in numerous ways, as folk culture, as high culture, as mass culture, and as popular culture. To find a single definition that will satisfy all is impossible and indeed pointless. What is of essential importance for this study is to develop an understanding of culture that does not separate it from the way it is created, produced, manufactured and distributed – what can be referred to as the system of production – in different social and economic systems. Consequently, the notion of the production of culture will be one of the central concerns of this study.

The conceptual confusion often surrounding the use of the term culture is clearly echoed in the use of the concepts of mass and popular culture. Lewis (1978), in a summary of the sociology of popular culture, observes that there has been little attempt at synthesis and a decided lack of agreement on basic terms and definitions. Indeed, according to Barbu (1976), the sociology of popular culture has not yet fulfilled the basic requirements of any systematic enquiry, a clear definition and a comprehensive classification. Thus in industrial societies the 'popular' metaphor is often used interchangeably with the 'mass' metaphor. What follows is an attempt at examining whatever consensus does exist for some key terms that are of use to us.

MASS CULTURE DEBATE

Mass culture is a term which has historically referred to the culture of the uneducated masses of industrial society. The term has been employed in academic research most often in two contexts: first, to describe the culture associated with the alienated masses of the post-war period (Riesman, 1951); and secondly to describe culture that is transmitted by the mass media (see Lewis, 1978). The first context is generally negative in its connotations, while the second context is limited by the fact that 'mass culture' has to be carried by the mass media.

Over the years two main lines have been taken in the mass culture 'debate'. The first is a 'critical' stance, while the second is a more 'positive' or 'pluralist' position. There are generally two types of critique directed at mass culture. The first is what we can call the 'conservative' critique, while the second is commonly referred to as the 'leftist' critique often represented by the Frankfurt School.

Both traditions view mass culture as transmitting distorted or false consciousness through the use of repetitive stereotypes and mechanical formulae. The effects of mass culture are a passive 'alienation' and 'anomie' amongst the mass audience, and to exclude the majority of people from active participation by manipulating an artificial consensus or 'lowest common denominator' of beliefs. Implicit in both the conservative and the Frankfurt School critiques is the judgement that the joint processes of industrialization and mass democracy, of which mass culture is a product, reinforce a rationalization and dehumanization of all forms of social and personal being into systems that destroy the autonomy of the majority while allowing a degree of individuality to privileged groups in society.

The most controversial account of mass culture and the music industry is that of Theodor Adorno. As Bradley (1981: 214) points out, 'with the contribution of Adorno to the social scientific study of music we enter the realm of the "great debate" about the quality and direction of contemporary culture as a whole'. Adorno's early writings stress the commodity character of popular music and its reifying effects, a topic which is also prominent in his later study of the culture industry with Horkheimer, the *Dialectic of Enlightenment*.

Horkheimer and Adorno argue that mass culture leads to homogenization. Standardization and mass production result in less variety of cultural forms available for audiences. Instead of new ideas, messages and values being expressed through art and music, there is a systematic reduction in the number of new ideas presented. As Koval (1988: 1) notes, the thrust of their argument is that 'old ideas are repeated over and over again in these media and thus culture is no longer characterized by diversity but is reduced to the repetition of a relatively narrow spectrum of forms and ideas which change slowly and with great resistance'. This continuous repetition of cultural form and content trivializes any meaning. Indeed they argue that

(Capitalist) culture consists of repetition. That its characteristic innovations are never anything more than improvements in mass production is not external to the system. It is with good reason that the interest of the innumerable consumers is directed to technique, and not to the contents – which are stubbornly repeated, outworn, and by now half-discredited.

(Horkheimer and Adorno, 1972: 134)

Thus any message that is repeated over and over loses any impact it may have had. For Horkheimer and Adorno it was in this way that culture loses its critical role in society: new and creative ideas are simply neutralized by incessant repetition and are thus absorbed into the capitalist order of things.

One side of the 'great debate' which roughly represents Adorno's view sees the existence of a worldwide working class, of more or less monopolistic industries producing cultural goods, and of increasing leisure time, which when taken together conspire to vulgarize, level, degrade and commercialize the culture of contemporary capitalist societies. The other side of the debate consists of the 'pluralists' who believe that the benefits of, for example, mass literacy, far outweigh any disadvantages, and that the availability of cheap cultural commodities is, in itself, not a bad thing.

According to Adorno (1941) popular music becomes standardized through the application of 'mechanical schemata' to its production. The standardization of commercial music aims at the standardization of audience reaction, of consumption, because it maximizes economic dividends. Driving Adorno's analysis is the suggestion of an ideological function in the process, to the effect that the standardization of musical consumption is part of an overall process aimed at making the consumer more malleable for the purpose of programmed consumption, not just of music but of everything else as well. Adorno also speaks of the reification and fetishization of music as it assumes a commodity form. Its fetishization refers to the irrational character taken on in the process of reification by aspects such as standardization, technique and authenticity in performance. According to Adorno, the process of reification eliminates the possibility of real or true pleasure, which is unthinkable for most modern researchers.

The thrust of Adorno's argument in the end was that the production of music as a commodity determined its cultural quality, that standardizing music produced its ideological effect. The mass production of cultural products could only result in a 'passive' consumption. The weakness of this argument, as Frith (1981) points out, is that it reduced consumption, a complex social process, to a simple psychological effect.

Walter Benjamin (1968), on the other hand, celebrated the positive possibilities of 'the work of art in the age of mechanical reproduction'. He argued that the technology of mass reproduction was a progressive force, through which the work of democratic artists could be shared with an audience in which everyone was able to be an 'expert' consumer. The technology of the mass media and mass reproduction had broken down traditional boundaries of authority and expertise by 'demystifying' the 'aura' surrounding art. The creation of cultural meaning was put back into the hands of the collective audience. Consequently, for Benjamin, the significance of cultural goods had become a matter of dispute, the ideological meaning of mass culture was decided in the process of consumption (see Frith, 1981).

Frith correctly points out that the critical accounts of popular music still depend on the Adorno–Benjamin positions. Out of Adorno have come the analyses of the economics of the entertainment industry in which the passivity function of commercial music-making is generally taken for granted. From Benjamin have come the subcultural theories of youth cultures making their own meaning, and creating through the process of consumption. This position is well represented today in the field of cultural studies (see Brake, 1980; Fiske, 1989; Hebdige, 1979, 1988; Willis, 1978, 1990).

Frith also reminds us that mass music is recorded music and records that don't sell don't enter the mass consciousness. Rock music is a mass medium and any analysis which claims it as folk or high art miss the point as a phonogram's ideological influence depends on what happens to it in the marketplace. Frith points out that the mass culture critics claim that he who controls the market controls the meaning and that the mass audience plays no part in cultural creation because even its markets are manipulated. This view makes no sense with regards to rock music according to Frith. The vast bulk of music aimed at the mass market simply never reaches it, thus, the industry is less organized around creating needs, than of responding to them. More often than not, the industry is following rather than leading taste.

INTRODUCING POPULAR CULTURE

Recently, to an increasing extent, scholars have begun to use the less value-laden term 'popular culture', which does not necessarily restrict usage to products of the mass media. Truzzi (1977) notes that popular culture transmission is usually indirect, via media and technology. It is available at moderate cost and is subject to copyright and patent laws. The norm is that standardized, formalized, multiple copies or performances are available. Producers and consumers are differentiated with major emphasis on mediators, especially in the area of product distribution. The product is consumer oriented and producers and mediators are mainly professionals (see Lewis, 1978).

Perhaps the most fundamental aspect of popular culture as a concept is that it is the product of industrialization. It is the advanced, urban, market economies that produce and shape the social relations and institutions in which popular culture as we know it can develop. Obviously then we are not using the term popular culture to describe the culture of the people, for it is equally obvious that all people in all societies have a culture. What is unique about popular culture has been characterized in the following attributes by Todd Gitlin (1981: 202):

1   centralized, corporate production (often multinational) and privatized consumption;
2   pervasiveness, and with it the potential for unifying the private domain with a 'new order of experience';
3   vast volume of output, structured obsolescence and rhythmic cycles of style and celebrity to maximize continuing turnover;
4   secularity, despite the ritualized form of many popular events, from sport to popular music.

For Gitlin, these attributes of popular culture enable it to be understood as a peculiarity of modern corporate capitalism, which in effect:

> presses popular culture into distinctive molds, and shapes it to particular uses ... These modern traits make it all the easier for popular culture to infuse everyday life, and to embody and reproduce the dominant complex of ideology: In the West, the legitimacy of private control of production, and of the national security state; the necessity of individualism, of status hierarchy, of consumption as the core measure of achievement; and overall, as in every society, the naturalness of the social order.
>
> (1981: 203)

From Gitlin's perspective, popular culture plays an important role in the reproduction of dominant values and social relationships in society. Popular culture has, in fact, an ideological function to fulfil.

A slightly different way of viewing popular culture is posited by Fiske (1989: 24) who claims that; 'popular culture is made by the people, not produced by the culture industry'. Popular culture is what people produce in their interaction with the products of the culture industries. Consequently, for Fiske, the key to understanding popular culture is to study the productive use of cultural commodities and not the production process. While this is a sympathetic approach, to simply ignore the production process is, at best, a perilous enterprise.

In approaching popular music as communication we are examining music as a facet of popular culture, or as one type of 'mass mediated culture'. The concept of mass mediated culture has been defined by Real (1977: 14) as encompassing 'expressions of culture as they arise from elite, folk, popular, or mass origins', and is based on the assumption that, 'all culture when transmitted by mass media becomes in effect popular culture'. Thus the cultural industries produce the popular culture that is distributed by the mass media.

The idea of 'cultural or culture industries' may at first glance seem like something of a contradiction in terms. Traditionally, 'culture' meant the high arts, and 'industry' was something to do with factories and wage labour. Cultural expression was the opposite of wage labour. When the Frankfurt School began to use the term 'culture industry', they did so to assert their general contempt for capitalism's use of the techniques of mass production and distribution to the realm of culture. Advances in theory and research have helped to create a broader understanding of the concept of culture. The previous distinction between 'high' culture (the arts) and 'low' or 'mass' culture (the media) have largely been broken down. As Sinclair (1992: 3) has noted, 'culture has now become the whole realm of ideas, images, symbols, objects and practices which make all of social life meaningful, however privileged or mundane its different levels may be'. Similarly, the concept of 'industry' has grown to refer to almost any area of productive activity. Prominent here are the relatively new forms of cultural production, in particular the audiovisual media: film, television, radio and recordings. For Sinclair, the scale, scope, stability, organization and export capabilities of some of these audiovisual media make the term 'industry' more than just an apt metaphor.

A broader definition of cultural industries, then, is those which produce goods or services which are either somehow expressive of the ways of life of a society, such as film, television and music, or which somehow occupy a special position within its system of social communication, such as advertising or the press. They are the industries which give form to social life in words and pictures, sounds and images. They increasingly offer the terms and symbols which we live our lives by.

POPULAR MUSIC

It is now necessary to change our focus and attempt to explain the way in which music fits into this framework. First it should be obvious that music can be part of all types of culture. What we need to do now is examine the use of the term 'popular music'. Just as with popular culture, popular music is often loosely used to denote a wide variety of musical styles and genres. The following represents the formulations most relevant to the present study.

For many scholars the key to understanding popular music is the idea of commercialization. In simplified terms, the goal of business is to strive for a product that maximizes profit. The music industry is no exception to this rule. When we speak of popular music we speak of music that is commercially oriented. This definition implies important connotations. In order to maximize one's profit one must achieve the greatest possible number of consumers. Record companies, musicians and radio stations are painfully aware of this fact and subsequently often try to orient their product so as to please as many as possible and thus maximize profit. McQuail (1986: 152) points out that 'more commercialism in mass communication inevitably intensifies competition for large audiences and, under conditions of channel "scarcity", leads to a neglect of those minority interests and tastes'.

Quantitatively, popular music is a recognized product. The number of records sold is measurable and observable. Popularity charts (e.g. Billboard) define what is being played on radio stations and selling in record stores. This amorphous market is quite distinct from others attuned to particular musical forms. Popular music is a much larger and eclectic idiom. Popular music is not just the sum total of all musical styles. It does not include all forms of music. Popular music is not beamed at all of the public but at a self-selected audience. This audience 'elects' what is popular with its listening time and dollars. Popular music then is a specific subcategory of the entire spectrum of music.

McPhee (1966) has likened the popular music marketplace with a voting arena. A music listener votes or registers her cultural choice by purchasing something, not just once per person but as many times as she pleases. We can suppose that the number of times one votes or purchases records is in proportion to how well she likes the existing fare in the cultural marketplace. Conversely, a person who does not like the existing fare will vote or purchase fewer records and thus becomes progressively disenfranchised. Where, as in political voting each person gets one vote, in cultural voting under commercial conditions the votes are numbers of people multiplied by their frequency of buying records. As McPhee notes, this helps to explain how a numerically small group (15 to 34 year olds) develop a much higher rate of consumption, its tastes are being better served, so that its total votes or purchases outnumber those of the numerically larger remaining possible audience.

For Denisoff (1975) popular music quantitatively consists of whichever musical styles sell sufficient numbers to be deemed successful or representative of an exoteric audience. Success is determined by indices of the music industry such as radio airplay and over the counter sales. Consequently, sufficient purchases by the youth audience, the main consumers, define what constitutes popular music at any specific time. The actual mechanics of the delineation of the youth market are highly complex. Youth tastes are not simply monolithic; they are shaped and influenced by numerous social forces around them ranging from age, race, marital status, sex, education and geographical location. In accepting that popular music is a whole that is different from the sum of its many diverse, static and dynamic parts, Denisoff (1975: 39), offers the following definition: 'Popular music is the sum total of those taste units, social groups and musical genres which coalesce along certain taste and preference similarities in a given space and time.'

Because these taste publics and genres are affected by so many factors the designation of popular music is seen by Denisoff as more of a sociological than a musical definition. People select what they like from what they hear. The reasons for this selection are influenced by many factors some of which have little to do with the aesthetic qualities of a particular song. As Denisoff observes, the record companies, 'must orchestrate this demographic cacophony in order to earn a profit'.

A musical definition of popular music is rife with difficulties. Robinson (1986) points out that the use of common musical qualities to define popular music is often impractical especially on an international level because the kinds of music that are popular vary from country to country. The problem is that some music is popular almost everywhere (pop music, rock music) while other music may be extremely popular in one country or region (reggae, salsa) and virtually unknown elsewhere.

Tagg (1982) distinguishes popular music from folk and art music according to: the nature of its distribution (usually mass distribution), the primary system used for its storage and distribution (recorded sound as opposed to either oral transmission or musical notation), the existence of its own musical theory and aesthetics and the relative anonymity of its composers. Tagg's socio-economic categories provide a better definition than most. They also establish popular music as a mass medium.

Tagg uses several additional descriptive divisions which Robinson (1986) points out are more problematic for an international definition of popular music. Tagg views popular music as usually occurring in industrial societies. However, popular music today appears in all types of societies even though it is primarily produced in urban, industrial centres. He also identifies popular music as financed mainly by free enterprise rather than public funding (as is the case with most art music) or as independent of the monetary system (as in the case of folk music). This differentiation, Robinson points out, ignores the socialist situation where popular music production, performance and distribution were often financed by the state (Wicke, 1984). It also raises questions about how to define locally produced music (for example, canto nuevo, which reaches a large number of people, is very popular, but is not highly commercialized or mass produced (Reyes Matta, 1982)). We can agree with Robinson that Tagg's parameters describe the usual, but not all instances, of popular music.

In summary, we can argue that popular music is self-defined, i.e. music that is popular. Popular music is directed at a self-selected audience. This audience essentially chooses or elects what is popular with its listening time and money. Thus, quantitatively, popular music is a recognized product. The number of records sold is measurable and observable. Numerous charts and hit lists in various countries define what is being played on radio stations and is selling in music stores.

This means that, for the music industry, popular music consists of whichever musical styles sell sufficient numbers to be deemed successful or representative of an audience. Success is determined by indices of the music industry such as radio play and phonogram sales. Consequently, sufficient purchases by the youth audience, the main consumers, define what constitute popular music at any given time. Keeping in mind that people's taste is by no means monolithic we can agree with Denisoff's above quoted definition of popular music.

MUSIC AND MASS COMMUNICATION

The study of music as mass communication has not emerged in the form of a coherent body of work. Musicologists and music historians have been mostly concerned with the technical description, evaluation and comparison of music. Ethnomusicologists have with varied success long been working to bring together anthropological and musicological methods. Sociologists of music have usually dealt with what we can call the musical branch of the mass culture debate. Some of these writers believe that music is best seen as articulating its social and cultural origins and thus likewise that its use by listeners must be viewed as a social practice related to other practices and determinations in their social life, and not simply derived from the music's 'message'.

Has music been studied as mass communication? The answer to this must be both yes and no. Music has been studied as the specific output of the mass medium of radio. In fact this tradition was developed by one of the founding fathers of modern communication studies, Paul Lazarsfeld, head of Columbia University's Radio Research Project in the 1940s. Together with Frank Stanton, who later became head of Columbia Broadcasting Systems (CBS), he helped to develop many of the empirical audience research techniques that were to be used for years by the broadcasting industry (Lazarsfeld and Stanton, 1941, 1944, 1949). Subsequent mass communication researchers have predominantly focused on the media's effects – the effects of television on children, newspapers on voters, advertising on consumers, popular music on children, and so on.

The study of the music industry is made especially difficult because of the fact that popular music crosses a range of different media – radio, cinema, television – as well as records, cassettes, compact discs, live performances and the music video. In each case it is conventionally employed in a range of ways, and plays an important part in linking and 'orchestrating' public and private cultures.

Music has seldom been studied as mass communication in its commodity form, phonograms. The problem is well formulated by Gronow (1983) as follows:

> Common sense tells us that sound recording – that is records and cassettes – is a mass medium just like newspapers, films or television. In industrialized countries, listening to records is just as much a part of everyday life as reading the newspaper or listening to the radio.
>
> A glimpse at standard textbooks on mass communication makes us doubt our common sense. Records are seldom mentioned at all, and certainly not considered as a medium comparable to film or radio.
>
> The problem is the message. The message of records is usually music, and communication research does not know how to deal with music. But musicologists have been equally blind to music as mass communication, and, as a consequence, the relatively few studies on the record industry which are available usually fail to consider this aspect.
>
> (Gronow, 1983: 53)

As Gronow argues, obviously a theory of mass communication which has nothing to say about that portion of broadcasting which consists of music, is in some ways inadequate, just as any theory of music which has nothing to say about the types of music which are most frequently communicated by the mass media must also be considered inadequate.

Phonograms are almost never included when discussions of the 'mass media' arise. Phonograms should not be ignored because the audience for a particular phonogram can number in the millions. In studying phonograms, we should want to know basic things about the medium that we already know about the other mass media. How large is the audience for phonograms? How many recordings are released and sold annually? How are phonograms produced, distributed and consumed? These and other questions will be taken up in this present study. It will also be suggested that level of phonogram sales is a very good indicator of the state of health of the music industry internationally.

For most people living in industrialized countries contact with music takes place mainly through mass media such as phonograms, radio, films and television. Music is routinely communicated across borders, often by transnational corporations. This relatively new situation requires a revision of standard models of musical communication. It will be argued that the development of the mass media has changed the nature of musical consumption as well as the types of music communicated.

As soon as there were media technically able to transmit sound, and communities economically able to use these media, there was mass communication of music. This occurred first with the development of the record industry, and was later followed by the development of radio, sound film, television and music video.

The history of the record industry suggests that the development of musical mass communications has to a large extent been determined by existing music communities in interaction with the media. The record industry has had to adapt itself to the realities of music far beyond its wishes. Music has probably influenced the record industry as much as the record industry has influenced music (see Gronow, 1980).

However these influences work in both directions. Recordings are a selective medium. Some types of music are more likely to be recorded than others. The record industry can also facilitate the diffusion of music from one community to another. Over time, both tendencies influence the musical life of communities that are increasingly dependent on the mass media for musical communication.

In recent decades the situation has changed considerably. In most countries often ten times as many recordings are sold today as in the 1950s. A much larger proportion of the world population today have access to a record, cassette or CD player as well as radios and televisions. Radio broadcasting relies on the music industry output as input and has become increasingly dependent on recorded music for a majority portion if its programme output. Recordings also influence music in films and on television, to say nothing of the new cultural commodity, the all pervasive music video. Also much of today's music has been created especially for recordings and is not necessarily ever performed live. The phonogram market has become more internationally oriented, and in many countries the majority of recordings sold are imported.

The phonogram is not only a means of communication and an art form. We must not lose sight of the fact that in a consumption oriented economy, music making is a business – well organized, capital intensive and unpredictable. A phonogram is often conceived, produced and marketed in much the same way as many other commodities. One could point to factors which seemingly separate phonograms from other products, but on closer examination many differences would prove illusory at best. The months, and occasionally years, of work involved in planning a phonogram are analogous to time devoted to styling of autos and to research on development of new generations of computers. Payments to key stars resemble remuneration to inventors in certain industries, while the copyright on a song is comparable to a copyright on a book or to a patent on an invention. The similarity runs even deeper because, like other commodities, the phonograms must be sold before they become obsolete. A music company executive remarked that, 'market segmentation, distribution, brand loyalty, new product launches . . . the industry fits quite neatly into the consumer goods category – especially if it is looked at from the top down'. Similarly an IFPI spokesman admitted that, 'in marketing terms the record business has always been relatively close to the type of business that Procter and Gamble does; the difference is that we are now acting as efficiently'.

A phonogram does have a quality, however, which sets it apart from many other marketable items. This is the distinction between overhead costs incurred in production and the incremental costs which are incurred when a phonogram is released. Virtually the entire cost of a phonogram occurs in making the original master tape. Securing an artist, hiring a producer and studio engineers, renting a studio, etc. – the expenses for all these are incurred in making the master tape. These are considered as overhead costs. The cost of a second phonogram is negligible compared to that of the first. The cost of a subsequent copy is the price of the raw stock/material, duplicating and pressing – the incremental costs. In these terms, the phonogram is a commodity one can duplicate indefinitely without substantially adding to the cost of the first unit produced. This is true whether the phonogram is a million dollar production or a cheap, home-studio-produced effort.

In the field of communication studies research into the cultural industries has usually been dealt with as part of the political economy of mass communications (see McAnany, 1985). It is generally only studied marginally or 'on the side' by internationally oriented researchers who are generally more interested in policy (e.g. Nordenstreng and Schiller, 1979; Schiller, 1981; Hamelink, 1983; Tunstall, 1986). The need to place problems in communication in historical perspective has been repeated time and time again. With regard to cultural industries, as pointed out above, there have already been many reviews of the expansion of transnational corporations into the world economy and of its impact on local as well as foreign economies. This large body of literature traces the general expansion of transnational, mainly American, companies into different economies around the world, during the 1960s and 1970s, and focuses on the US as the major world power culturally, which is not meant to imply a conspiracy theory, 'but is as objective an assessment as possible of the logical consequences of the world economic system that has traditionally distributed primary products, industrial goods, and capital for centuries, but only in the twentieth century has begun to distribute entertainment, news, information, and educational messages on an increasingly global scale' (McAnany, 1985: 4). This system is characterized as asymmetrical in the distribution of power accorded to a few dominant economic centres. The cumulative body of research suggests that 'the study of cultural industries goes beyond formalist analyses of the cultural products themselves to a better understanding of how the process of production influences and is influenced by the themes embodied in the products' (McAnany, 1985: 10).

At this point we have in effect come full circle and can sum up with once again returning to Adorno. While much of Adorno's work is considered vulgar by contemporary standards, to simply disregard him is to belittle his contribution to the study of popular music as mass communication. The major strength of Adorno's work is that he attempted to understand the total musical field by examining the surrounding complex socio-musical world. He envisioned their common commoditization by the new means of mass reproduction. Remarkably, until recently, Adorno stood alone in the history of socio-cultural studies in addressing contemporary music as a totality.

Jacques Attali (1985) is the first to seriously take up Adorno's challenge and study the socio-musical totality, albeit from a very different direction. He utilizes a meta-theoretical analysis in which music is a herald, 'for change is inscribed in noise faster than it transforms society'. Music is a 'prophetic indicator' in two ways: 'in its compositional procedures –

the ways in which the violence of noise is channeled or formally controlled – and in the modes of producing, distributing and consuming music' (Attali, 1985: 56). In theorizing through music he proposes to use music as a medium through which to read history. For it is music that, 'simulates the social order, and its dissonances express marginalities. The code of music simulates the accepted rules of society (ibid.: 29).

Attali sketches four different musical eras in history. The first stage is *sacrifice*, characterized by the ritual practices of sacred societies. This is an era before exchange value when music is purely social and ritual. Attali claims that in this era, 'the production of music has as its function the creation, legitimation and maintenance of order ... Music ... constitutes the collective memory and organizes society' (ibid.: 30).

The second stage is *representation*, in which music making is a professional activity tied to the marketplace, with music itself being a commodity but still as live performance. This is the era when money enters society and music is commoditized and labour is valorized. Thus music is 'employed to make people believe ... that there is order in exchange and legitimacy in commercial power' (ibid.: 19).

The third stage, *repetition*, is the era of the recording, when music as commodity is endlessly reproduced, with live performance reduced in importance and the creation of demand primary. This is the era of capitalism, mass production and mass reproduction. Thus people must work to produce the means to purchase recordings, the result being that, 'people buy more records than they can listen to. They stockpile what they want to find the time to hear' (ibid.: 101). Thus use-time and exchange-time destroy one another.

The fourth stage, *composition*, is a utopian sketch of a possible future in which people will make their own music, for themselves, in a free and decentralized society. Attali foresees a 'new way of doing music ... Doing music for the sake of doing' (ibid.: 134).

What is interesting for the present study is Attali's ability to connect music with the prevailing forms of production, distribution and consumption in a given era. As will be discussed below, studying the systems of production and consumption is essential to the understanding of the role of popular culture in contemporary society. Clearly, in terms of Attali's categorization scheme, we find ourselves with the present study in the third stage, that of repetition. It is the organization and structure of that repetition that we shall turn to in the following chapters. But first an observation from Herbert Schiller who notes that:

The last fifty years have seen an acceleration in the decline of non-market-controlled creative work and symbolic output. At the same time, there has been a huge growth in its commercial production. Parallel with the private appropriation of symbolic activity has been the rationalization of its production. This includes the development of more efficient techniques and the invention of means to expand the market output to a global scale. The production of goods and services in the cultural sphere has indeed been industrialized. It is in this respect that the term 'cultural industries' assumes its meaning.

(Schiller, 1989: 32)

Schiller claims that the expanded production and distribution capabilities have greatly increased the profitability of cultural production, although this is seldom discussed when attention is instead focused upon the capabilities of the new technologies. While the profitability of new technologies is seldom denied, the often quoted increase in programme diversity is seldom demonstrated. This certainly poses a special problem when trying to illuminate the process of cultural production and consumption on today's global scale.

Chapter 4

The music industry in transition

> A change to a new type of music is something to beware of as a hazard of all our fortunes. For the modes of music are never distributed without unsettling of the most fundamental political and social conventions.
>
> (Plato, *The Republic*)

In Chapter 4 we shall examine the transition taking place in the contemporary international music industry. Worldwide sales figures are presented to highlight some recent international trends. I will also discuss the main actors in the international music industry.

AN INDUSTRY IN TRANSITION

The phonogram industry has been 'international' for some time now. As Gronow (1983) has perceptively noted, the industry can be historically divided into three important 'expansion' periods. The first was prior to the First World War, a time when the industry developed many of its present day working structures and established itself around the world.

The second expansion period took place in the late 1920s, only to end with the onset of the depression. Following the depression radio and film took over the prominent position that recordings had held.

The third expansion period started in the late 1950s and ended in the late 1970s. During this time record sales grew rapidly throughout the industrialized countries and the phonogram became an established medium worldwide. Gronow further suggests that recordings, as a mass medium, have now reached a saturation point, hence the lack of real sales growth in the industrialized world.

Any contemporary work on the international music industry must therefore take into account the downturn of industry sales in the late 1970s. This 'crisis' hit the industry after more than 30 years of constant growth.

The 1970s were particularly a period of exceptional growth with the value of worldwide record sales rising from $4.75 billion to $7 billion between 1973 and 1978 (IFPI). According to Frith (1988b) the year of truth was 1979, when music sales fell by 11 per cent in the USA, and by 20 per cent in Britain. This decline continued unabated until 1982 and not before 1984 were total sales figures in dollars back at 1979 levels. In 1988, when money sales in both the USA and the UK were the highest in the history of the industry, the total number of units sold was still below the 1978 level (from 726 million to 672 million in the USA).

The industry reaction to all this has been one of confused caution at best. While at times claiming that 'boom time' was back due to the popularity of music television and the successful marketing of the compact disc, most executives would agree with *Billboard*'s 1984 editorial that any 'recovery' was 'due more to the runaway success of a handful of smash hits than to an across the board pickup' in sales. At the same time that the 'recovery' was supposedly happening, Frith (1988b) pointed out that CBS cut its worldwide payroll from 17,160 employees in 1980 to 10,110 in 1986.

In summing up the period since the early 1980s several trends or patterns seem to have emerged. Except for a slight decline in 1982, world sales of phonograms (records, prerecorded cassettes, CDs) have steadily increased after the 'crisis' from approximately $12 billion in 1981 to $29 billion in sales in 1992. Sales of long play albums and singles have plummeted drastically and continue to do so. In 1992 vinyl album sales were down to 126 million units, less than a seventh of the amount from 1981 when 1.2 billion units were sold. Singles have declined by 40 per cent over the decade but have started to show increased sales due to the introduction of the single cassette and single compact disc. The formats that have increased in sales and sustained industry growth are the long play prerecorded cassette and the compact disc. Over the decade, cassette sales have tripled while the growth of the compact disc has been meteoric. In 1992 some 1.152 billion compact discs were sold compared to 260 million in 1987. Cassettes are now the most popular sound carriers worldwide with some 1.551 billion units sold in 1992 (IFPI, 1993). World sales by format are shown in Figure 4.1.

One definite article of faith amongst industry people is that the compact disc has saved the industry. First, CDs revived consumer interest in music and allowed companies to resell their back catalogues; and, second, they enabled companies to increase the price of their products (Burnett, 1990a). In the USA, CD sales took off in 1985 and by 1990, for every album sold, six compact discs and thirteen prerecorded cassettes were sold. This is a

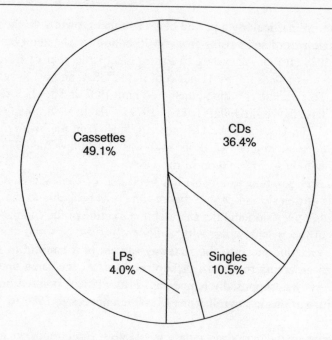

Figure 4.1 World sales by format, 1992

Source: IFPI

trend that industry executives expect will happen in most countries. It is important to see the rise of the CD in its proper context, as part of the overall transformation of the music industry. The transnational firms are now in the business of selling their music across the globe. Along with the continuing deregulation of national television and radio services, the increase of new cable and satellite delivery services, and the spread of VCRs, has grown the demand for programme material. Music, in all its different forms, has proven to be an important source of programme 'content', enabling the industry to pre-sell programme material for the first time (Frith, 1988b). The 1990s will see the industry move away from the selling of products to concentrate on the selling of musical rights and the collecting of royalties (Wallis, 1991). Given the increasing exploitation of sound recordings by broadcasters, it is clear that in the future, income generated from publishing and performance rights will have to constitute an equally increasing part of record company revenues.

Within the industry itself there is a clear picture of where things are going and what the rest of the 1990s will entail. In a recent interview the president of the International Federation of Phonogram and Video

Producers (IFPI), Mr Menon, outlined the move towards the selling of musical rights and the collecting of royalties:

> Over the last decade new means of distribution such as satellite trans-missions and interactive cable broadcasting systems have exposed the consumer to far greater access to sound recordings. Given the increasing exploitation of sound recordings by broadcasters, it is clear that in the future, income generated from performance rights must constitute an equally increasing part of record company revenues, and IFPI will seek to ensure that transfrontier transmissions are covered by adequate copyright law and fair remuneration to producers. The revolution that is transforming the growing deregulated broadcasting landscape must provide record companies, performers, musicians, publishers and authors with proper levels of reward for the use of their works.
>
> (IFPI, 1990)

Just who will be competing to share these rewards is already well known. A top Warner's executive offered the following scenario:

> For better or for worse, the wave of the 90s will be huge, well financed companies that are involved in 4 or 5 forms of entertainment, and where competition is not other US companies but Sony in Japan and Bertelsmann in Germany.
>
> (*Herald Tribune*, 27 October 1989)

Before examining these transnational actors on the music scene we shall first have a look at the size of the international marketplace for phonograms.

THE SIZE OF THE INTERNATIONAL MARKET

The structure of an industry has to do with the number and relative size of firms in the market producing cultural products. To put this into perspective we must first establish the size of the international music industry. This will help us to understand the scope of the major trans-national music companies and thus enable us to examine the typical operations of these different types of companies and how they interact in order to describe the structure and operations of the contemporary inter-national music industry.

The musical cultural commodities produced by the international music industry are an increasingly global concern, making the music industry quite likely the most transnational of all the culture industries. As the number of sales has levelled off in the crucial American marketplace since

Table 4.1 World sales of phonograms: top ten territories by share of world market, 1992 (million units and per cent market share)

USA	8866.6	31.1
Japan	4328.5	15.2
Germany	2636.9	9.2
UK	1998.2	7.0
France	1935.4	6.8
Canada	861.7	3.0
Italy	653.8	2.3
Netherlands	647.4	2.3
Spain	586.7	2.0
Australia	492.4	1.7

Source: IFPI

reaching saturation point in 1978 (Burnett and Weber, 1989), the major companies have increasingly looked outwards internationally for new markets. By the mid-1980s CBS, WEA, EMI and Polygram were all claiming in their annual reports that their international divisions accounted for more than half of their sales.

In 1992 the total sales of the international music industry (as registered by IFPI members) were approximately $29 billion. Table 4.1 lists the 1992 total sales of prerecorded music in the largest markets as well as the estimated percentage share of the world market.

Table 4.1 shows that the United States is the largest market with sales of $8,866 billion. The only other countries with sales over $1 billion in 1992 were Japan (4,328), Germany (2,636), the United Kingdom (1,998) and France (1,935). The next group of countries, ranked by sales in millions of dollars included Canada (861), Italy (653), Netherlands (647), Spain (586) and Australia (492). Smaller but still important markets were Argentina (184), Austria (288), Belgium (320), Brazil (262), China (320), Denmark (192), Finland (135), India (254), Norway (232), Poland (64), Portugal (74), Russia (150), South Korea (471), Sweden (201), Switzerland (321), Taiwan (326), and Thailand (159). The rest of the world accounts for the remaining percentage of global sales. It is important to observe that, if measured in terms of total units instead of dollars, countries like Russia, India and China would be placed much higher up the list.

Sales figures released show that in 1988 for the first time, the total values of sales in the European Community ($6,282 million) was higher than that in the USA ($6,254 million). However, the United States remained the largest single market in the world and more units (LPs, CDs, cassettes) were sold in the USA (672 million) than in the EC (549 million).

In 1992 it was estimated that total sales in the EC accounted for approximately 35 per cent of world sales while the United States accounted for 32 per cent.

DEVELOPMENTS OBSERVED

What do we know about popular music as a process of international communication? What can we say about why Anglo-American popular music is apparently so much more 'popular' than that of other countries? What do we know about the distribution of popular music on the international level? The answer to all of these questions is, of course, not very much.

This echoes the remarks of Malm (1982) who reflects that:

Considering the fact that sound recordings have been in existence for over one hundred years and have been an important mass medium since the 1920s, surprisingly little research has been done on them. Few attempts have been made to summarize what is known about the general importance of sound recordings in society as a whole and the world of music in particular.

(Malm, 1982: 49)

We do know that record companies are generally described not only in terms of their size but in terms of the degree of control they have over their product. Currently there are three main types of company within the international phonogram industry. Traditionally, these companies have been described as follows. First there are the transnationals or majors, who control the lion's share of the market, manufacture and distribute their own product. They are vertically integrated multinationals, and combine the commissioning and contracting of artists, with their own recording studios, the technologies needed to press and package records, and a sophisticated marketing, promotion and distribution network worldwide.

Second, there are the middle tier or minors, smaller companies who tend to gain their share of the market by making production and distribution deals with the majors, or with independent studios, presses and production and distribution facilities. Most of the minors are now controlled by the transnationals as we will see below.

Third, are the 'alternative labels' or 'indies' which operate less conventionally than the majors through a network of independent, often short-term contacts and contracts. They place their emphasis on cheapness of production and often have localized networks of production and distribution. They often open up access to forms of music not catered for or contained within the mainstream music market. Many of these new independents developed around existing independent recording studios who decided to establish their own recording labels, representing groups and types of music to which they were committed, but which were ignored by the majors.

Due to the special nature of phonograms and the process of production there are no official reliable statistics on production currently available. The production of phonograms is estimated to exceed the transnationality of all other types of cultural production. Because of relatively low production costs it is possible for the transnational record companies to produce in several countries. In order to estimate the transnational flow of phonograms it is best to approach the market from the point of view of consumption rather than production, because the music industry as well as the music trade journals produce ample information on the consumption of records, cassettes and compact discs (see Mowlana, 1986).

For books or films it is relatively easy to compile statistics based on a single unit, one book or one film. In recorded music the single unit, an LP or a single, is really only useful for best seller charts or hit lists, which have a continuously changing character. A better idea can be obtained by studying, for instance, the market shares of various record companies in different hit parades in different countries over a given period of time. The study of hit parades over longer periods of time gives an idea where the best selling records come from. The sales of popular music represent at least 80 per cent of the total sales of records in most countries (IFPI, 1990), hence the sales of classical music, for example, cannot change the general market pattern, although a Pavarotti occasionally makes the best seller charts.

THE ACTORS: TRANSNATIONALS TAKE CONTROL

There are six firms in the international music industry that can be defined as transnational phonogram companies. One is American owned (Warner), two are Japanese (Sony, MCA), one is German (BMG), one is British (EMI) and one is Dutch owned (Polygram). Each of these major firms is itself a division of an even larger electronics or communications conglomerate. BMG Music, formerly RCA, was until 1986 a division of the American electronics giant, Radio Corporation of America/General Electric. It is now owned by the German, Bertelsmann Music Group (BMG) which in turn is a division of the world's largest publisher, the

Bertelsmann Publishing Group. EMI records is a division of the Thorn–EMI electronics corporation, while the majority of Polygram is owned by the Philips electronic corporation. Warner Music is a division of the communication giant, Time Warner. Sony Music was previously CBS records, a division of the broadcasting conglomerate Columbia Broadcasting Systems until late 1987 when it was sold to the Japanese Sony electronics corporation. MCA was bought by the Japanese Matsushita company in 1990. All six of the phonogram majors have branch subsidiaries throughout Europe and the Americas. An oligopoly exists in the international market today with the six transnationals controlling the majority of the market. The strong trend towards concentration is a situation long acknowledged in the industry.

In 1977 a prominent industry executive proclaimed:

> One of the key trends of the next decade will be the increasing concentration of market shares in the hands of a few large manufacturing/distribution concerns. The record industry shows the classic signs of a mature industry as weaker companies are gradually bought out or fold ... Soon an oligopoly will exist in our industry.
>
> (*Billboard*, 1977: 32)

As will be seen below, this has indeed become the case. We will now turn to a short historical description of the main actors in the transnational industry.

Sony Music

Sony Music is the world's largest record company with an annual worldwide turnover of over $3 billion. In December 1987 the Japanese consumer electronics corporation Sony paid $2 billion to purchase the CBS Records division from its American parent company Columbia Broadcasting Systems Inc. At the time of sale, music, including music publishing, accounted for just over 25 per cent of the corporation's total turnover; broadcasting for approximately 40 per cent. In addition to seven book publishing companies and more than 60 magazines, CBS subsidiaries included toy manufacturing, Steinway pianos, Fender guitars and Rogers drums.

CBS got started in the record industry in 1938 when it bought the Columbia Phonograph Co., which was founded in 1888. Columbia Records soon rivalled RCA as America's biggest label. It developed into a major international company in the 1960s and in 1965 formed CBS Records International as an umbrella organization for the company's international operations. Due mainly to its complex corporate structure, CBS had a reputation for being staid, impersonal and very bureaucratic (Qualen, 1985). Denisoff comments:

> CBS Records, with its plant and catalog, must produce an enormous amount of products to keep its various bureaus, agencies and departments busy. Of every ten records released, only two or three will sell. Consequently, large companies must produce massive amounts of product to sustain their larger corporate bodies.

> (Denisoff, 1975: 97)

It is important to note that in its new corporate home, music accounts for only about 11 per cent of Sony's total corporate turnover. Sony Music has branch plants in over 40 countries. North America is its biggest market, representing 50 per cent of total sales. Europe accounts for 30 per cent, while Japan for another 10 per cent of world sales.

Warner Music

Warner Music is the music division of Time Warner Inc., the result of the 1989 merger between American-owned Time and Warner Communications. Warner Music is thus the outcome of a number of mergers. The beginning of Warner's record production was in 1958 when the Warner Bros movie company formed a record label, Warner Bros Records. Warner took over Reprise Records in 1964. Warner and Reprise comprise one of three Warner subsidiaries in the field of record production, the other two being Atlantic (acquired in 1967) and Elektra/Asylum (acquired in 1970–1972). These three subsidiaries are distributed in the USA by the WEA Corporation and in the rest of the world by Warner Communications International (formed 1981). Warner Communications also includes movie, television and publishing interests, Atari Inc., Knickerbocker Toy Company, major shares in Coca-Cola, major shares in Bausch and Lamb Optical and several US cable TV companies.

Warner's specialized production has traditionally impeded the company's growth internationally. Its foreign branches have not been very active in producing recordings of national artists of different countries. The parent companies' restrictive production policies is reflected in the lack of success internationally in the 1970s. Warner is currently trying to increase the role of local product in the catalogues of its foreign branches.

Warner's most important marketing areas are the English-speaking countries, USA, Canada, UK, Australia and New Zealand. Warner is forming numerous foreign branches, especially in Europe, Asia and some developing countries. Warner is the fastest growing transnational record company internationally with sales tripling between 1975 and 1990. Of all the transnationals, Warner Communications is the most media and software oriented. Thus its turnover has been the most volatile as its various divisions have prospered or suffered, depending on changing market conditions. Music accounts for approximately 25 per cent of its sales and films for 30 per cent, but because of the corporation's deep involvement in film these proportions can change significantly year to year on the basis of blockbuster successes or flops (Qualen, 1985).

The former CEO of Time Warner, Steve Ross, in an interview outlined his 'global strategy' arguing that 'the world is our public' (*Financial Times*, 10 April 1990). Warner has been active in buying European independent labels, including Metronome (Sweden), Magnet (UK), Teldec (Germany), CGD (Italy) and Carrere and Erato (France).

Thorn–EMI

Thorn–EMI is the result of the 1980 merger of the two British firms, Thorn Electronics and EMI Records. EMI was formed in 1931 as a result of a merger between the Columbia Gramophone Co. (UK branch of American Columbia Phonogram Co.) and the Gramophone Co. (founded in London 1898). Columbia and Gramophone continued to compete until they took the common EMI name in the 1960s. Before the Second World War, EMI controlled most European record companies and was responsible for the majority of European-produced records.

After the Second World War, the boom in popular music meant above all the expansion of American artists and products. EMI relied mainly on licence deals with American companies for success. Thus EMI marketed American products both in the UK and on the continent. In 1955 EMI entered the American market by acquiring the Capitol company (formed 1942). In 1954 EMI sold its radio and gramophone manufacturing interests to Thorn. In 1969 EMI acquired the Associated British Picture Corporation (ABPC) and thus Thames Television (Frith, 1981).

In 1979 EMI acquired the American United Artists record company. Ironically in 1980, 25 years after selling to Thorn, EMI itself was bought in its entirety by Thorn. Music now accounts for some 28 per cent of Thorn–EMI total turnover. The merger of the hardware oriented Thorn and the software-oriented EMI was clearly planned with an eye to the video and cable revolution. Thorn–EMI was an early owner of the now defunct Music Box satellite channel. Thorn–EMI can now produce the hardware to go along with the software.

Thorn–EMI's current markets include approximately 30 per cent of sales in Europe and 20 per cent of sales in North America. As a result of its 'imperial' past and subsidiaries formed in the 1920s, Thorn–EMI also has a strong foothold in the expanding Asian markets, with even a manufacturing plant in Peking (Hardy, 1985). EMI owns the Pathé label in France as well as Electrola in Germany. Recent EMI purchases have been Minos Matsas (Greece), Hispavox (Spain), Chrysalis (UK) and Virgin (UK). The purchase of Virgin Music Group was particularly interesting. Virgin was established in 1970 as a UK mail order record company by Richard Branson. Virgin soon moved into record production, and opened record stores that have grown into a major chain. In the 1980s Virgin had diversified into youth culture-related activities such as films, music videos, books, and a transatlantic airline company (Qualen, 1985). The purchase of the Virgin Music Group, the last of the major independent labels, brought such stars as the Rolling Stones and Janet Jackson under the EMI umbrella. The first thing EMI did after purchasing Virgin was to lay off 450 of Virgin's 1,200 employees and cut its artistic roster nearly in half.

In a further attempt to strengthen the company position in the field of music, EMI purchased the SBK Entertainment World, a publishing company, and also another major music publisher, the Filmtrax Copyright Holding corporation. EMI Music president Jim Fifield then named SBK Records president Charles Koppelman CEO of EMI North America. Koppelman responded by firing the president of Capitol (EMI's American label) as well as 60 employees, and making cuts in the artistic roster.

Since becoming president of EMI Music, Fifield's aggressive acquisition spree has included spending $121 million for Chrysalis Records, $26 million for SBK Records, and $297 million for SBK Entertainment World, all in 1989. In 1992 EMI spent $960 million to purchase the Virgin Music Group. These moves have won EMI 15 per cent of the global music market, and EMI is just slightly behind the industry's Big Three: Warner Music, Sony Music Entertainment and Polygram.

Polygram

Polygram is a management and holding company originally based on the interlocking relationship of Phonogram (owned by the Dutch Philips Electrical) and Polydor (owned by Deutsche Grammophon, which is a subsidiary of the German electrical corporation Siemens). It is Phonogram

International and Polydor International that produce and market records under the Polygram umbrella. Thus Polydor plus Phonogram equals Polygram. The Philips organization bought out the Siemens share of Polygram and consequently now controls the company.

In 1898 the British Gramophone Company established a German branch called Deutsche Grammophon. In 1917 Deutsche Grammophon became an independent company and in 1924 started using the Polydor name outside Germany. In 1941 Siemens bought the company. Philips started in the record business in 1950 and in 1962 the Siemens–Philips merger took place. In 1972 they adopted the company name, Polygram.

Polygram's labels include the Phonogram-controlled, Philips, Vertigo, Mercury, and the Polydor-controlled, Deutsche Grammophon, Polydor and MGM. In 1976 Polygram bought the RSO (Robert Stigwood Organization) record and movie company. In 1978 Polygram bought into Barcley, France's largest record company. In addition, Polygram took over Decca, the renowned British firm, and bought a majority of shares in Casablanca (records and movies) all in 1980 (Soramäki and Haarma, 1981).

Polygram is today, a transnational of the music industry, involved on a world scale in manufacturing, production, marketing and distribution as well as publishing. The Polygram annual report well defines the extent of the organization as a major company 'which has affiliates in 31 countries ... employs 13,000 people ... has facilities (manufacturing) in 20 countries'. Polygram has gone on a spending spree in Scandinavia and purchased Polar Music (Sweden) and Sonet (Sweden).

Polygram, in a bid to boost its historically weak position in the US market (a problem it shares with EMI and BMG), bought A&M Records in 1989 and Island Records in 1990. A significant presence in the American market is vital to all the transnationals since it represents by far the single most important music market in the world. A Polygram executive motivated the reasons for buying both A&M and Island for a total of $732 million, because 'Polygram was deficient in the American rock market'. Polygram is also significantly into film production as well as television and music video specials.

Island Records was formed by Chris Blackwell in 1962 to distribute Jamaican record labels in the UK. Island has grown steadily with the reputation of being *the* progressive rock label. In the 1970s Island attempted to expand by buying its own pressing plant and distributing its own product. This expansion failed and soon Island was back to relying on the transnationals for the manufacturing and distribution of its products (Qualen, 1985). A&M Records was founded in 1962 by Herb Alpert and Gerry Moss (A&M), as a means of initially promoting Alpert's own records. To this day it still operates exclusively in the record and music industry. A&M has been most successful in the United States and only recently internationally.

Polygram also acquired the US distribution rights .to Motown in 1991, and took the logical step of buying the label outright in 1993 from MCA and Diana Ross's Boston Ventures company who had purchased the label in 1988 from owner Berry Gordy. Polygram, in purchasing the 'Motown sound', bought what is one of the most valuable pop music catalogues in the business. Gordy who sold the company to MCA in 1988 retained the lucrative publishing rights to Motown's old songs for his Jobete Music Company. The deal, which cost Polygram an estimated $300 million, includes Motown's music division, TV, film and video production, and the marketing department. Also included was the copyright to the Motown name.

The president of Philips, Jan Timmers, in commenting on the relationship between the recording industry and the consumer electronics industry confirmed 'that the music hardware and software industries exist in symbiosis – which, according to my dictionary, means: The intimate living together of two dissimilar organisms in a mutually beneficial relationship' (IFPI, 1991).

Bertelsmann Music Group (BMG)

The Bertelsmann Music Group (BMG) is a division of one of the world's largest media conglomerates, the German Bertelsmann Publishing Group. Bertelsmann Music Group (BMG) became a transnational player by purchasing American RCA records in 1986. RCA entered the record industry in 1928 when it acquired the Victor Talking Machine corporation, at one time the largest manufacturer of records and gramophones in the USA. RCA did its best business in the 1930s and 1940s when it rivalled Columbia as the top American label. In the last two decades it has achieved a powerful international position.

The RCA Record company was under the umbrella of the giant Radio Corporation of America (RCA) which was founded after the Second World War by American Telephone and Telegraph, Western Electric, General Electric and Westinghouse. RCA is a leader in electronics, the parent company of the NBC television network, and the owner of six book publishing companies, including Random House, Alfred Knopf, Pantheon Books, Vintage Books, Modern Library and Ballantine Books (Nelson, 1979). The role of RCA in rock music has been described by Chapple and Garofalo (1977) as follows:

RCA ... is the corporate giant that 'missed the boat' ... on both fifties rock 'n' roll and sixties rock. RCA latched onto Elvis Presley and the Jefferson Airplane, top sellers in their periods, but nevertheless estimated that both rock 'n' roll and progressive rock were just fads. The weakness of the company has been its inability to react to changes in mainstream rock music ... It has never been able to regard significant new music as music. The rapid turnover of top executives, the underuse of outside producers, and the old fashioned approach to advertising have reinforced the company's distance from the music. RCA represents the way old-line bureaucratic corporations deal with creativity.

(Chapple and Garofalo, 1977: 209)

BMG has been conservative because of its close ties with the parent company. In order to function well within the record industry, a company needs an organizational structure that will allow for rapid adjustments to ever changing market conditions. Thus the tight framework imposed on the BMG record label may have lessened its capacity for adapting to an ever changing market.

BMG has updated its production and marketing capacity and made major changes within management. These changes have been directed at improving the company's position in the rock market. In this regard BMG has in the 1980s acquired both the European Ariola–Eurodisc label and the American Arista Records which was originally formed in 1974 by Columbia Motion Pictures. BMG has purchased the Record Station (Sweden) and Genlyd (Denmark) labels.

Bertelsmann has 44,000 employees in 30 countries, the publishing (books, magazines) and record industries are its principal activities in the global marketplace. As a BMG executive expressed the international strategy: 'while increasing in complexity and becoming even more fiercely competitive, this sector of the economy will continue to grow. Success will depend on skill, experience and creativity in each market segment and – to the extent that entertainment properties of international importance are involved – a global infrastrucure.'

MCA Music Entertainment

MCA Music Entertainment is the newest transnational and a result of the Japanese electronics giant, Matsushita's purchase of the MCA media company in 1990. Matsushita also gained control of MCA Movies and Universal Studios.

Table 4.2 Music sales as % of parent companies' total sales, 1992

	%
Time Warner	24
Thorn–EMI	28
Bertelsmann	21
Sony	11
Philips	10
Matsushita	8

Source: Company reports

MCA (Movie Corporation of America) is part of a corporate structure similar to the former RCA. Movies are MCA's major business with records accounting for only about 10 per cent of sales. MCA entered the record business in 1956 by purchasing American Decca, a subsidiary formed in 1934 by the British Decca Company. This enabled MCA to hold a fairly strong position in the market in the late 1950s and 1960s. In 1979 MCA acquired ABC's record division which was founded in 1956. This acquisition was seen as an attempt to expand more directly into the rock music market. MCA is establishing a number of international subsidiaries. For example, in the late 1970s MCA began to distribute both the independent labels, Chrysalis and IRS, worldwide.

MCA's first major move was the 1988 takeover of the famous Motown record company. MCA paid $61 million for Motown. Commenting on the takeover, Berry Gordy, Motown's founder and owner, had the following to say: 'In today's economy the big get bigger while the small disappear. By selling to MCA we can at least guarantee releasing records' (*Variety*, 1988).

Motown was founded in 1960 in Detroit by Berry Gordy. Motown was the only major record company with black ownership in the history of the American music industry. Motown has the industry image as 'the black record company' with almost exclusively black executives and artists. The Motown 'sound' has been successful worldwide. The company production is oriented exclusively towards rhythm 'n' blues and soul music of the black community. This has been the company's strength as well as its weakness in the international market.

MCA posted more than $325 million in Domestic (American) sales in 1992, making it the top year in its history. Industry sources claim that David Geffen personally collected $750 million in cash when he sold Geffen Records to MCA. This could be part of the reason why MCA turned around and sold Motown to Polygram in 1993. For purposes of comparison Table 4.2 presents the music sales of the six transnationals as the percentage of the parent corporations' total sales. Here we see that music sales are an important source of revenue for Time Warner, Thorn–EMI and Bertelsmann, while of less importance for Sony, Philips and Matsushita.

INDEPENDENT AND ALTERNATIVE COMPANIES

There are literally hundreds of independent record companies operating in most countries in our sample. The independents operate less conventionally than the majors through a network of independent, often short-term, contacts and contracts. These independents place their emphasis on cheapness, and often have localized networks of production and distribution. For example, in Sweden several independent labels manufacture and distribute their records through the jointly owned MD distribution company. In the UK, Pinnacle distributes the music of solely independent labels. Jet distribution performed a similar role in the American market.

A key factor in the development of the independent sector was provided by cheaper, more compact and efficient technologies for recording music, which also carried implications for established professional production companies. The independents must often cope with living between the need to operate within a commercial market, and a desire to innovate. As Elliot notes: 'Although they all obviously had commercial motives, they were equally concerned with making a new type of music – and a new type of production system – more widely available' (Elliot, 1982: 29).

There is a clear relationship between size and profitability in the music industry. The gap between the transnationals and the independents has become even more pronounced. The independent sector has mushroomed on the back of new technology, only to be decimated by the combined effects of acquisition and recession, in addition to soaring distribution expenses. What costs a lot is not cutting a disc but promoting it. As a result, some independents have concentrated on dance music, which is played in clubs rather than on the air. If the DJs push a record it can establish an artist on the special dance music charts which is far less costly than trying to break into the mainstream sales charts.

The independents have also been unable to benefit from the premium profit market in CD sales. By squeezing vinyl out of the market, the majors have also effectively eliminated the independents. In fact, the potential for recycling old releases in digital formats helps to explain the willingness of the big music companies to pay large sums for established companies such as Motown. The absence of any back catalogues on which they can cash in puts the newer independents at a disadvantage. The problem is likely to become still more acute with the development of new digital applications. The potential for transmitting via cables, satellite or telephone lines means that home listeners will have access to the equivalent of a *global jukebox*. Subscribers to the digital networks connect a receiver to their own stereo systems to get dozens of channels of uninterrupted CD sound. With such advances on the horizon, the value of the transnationals tying up valuable back catalogues becomes clear.

In a study of phonogram industry concentration (Burnett, 1992b) the transnationals were found to dominate the market in the United States, the United Kingdom, Canada, Germany, Italy, Australia, Sweden, Japan, France and The Netherlands. When the total market shares of the transnationals was taken into account (own labels, licensing, distribution), there were five countries (UK, Italy, Japan, Sweden, France) where the transnationals had between 60 and 80 per cent of the total market shares. In the rest of the sample the transnationals controlled over 80 per cent of the market shares.

It is important to note that the transnationals dominate the market in big countries as well as small; in English-speaking countries as well as non-English-speaking countries. It should be emphasized that this domination is based on the partnerships which the transnationals have with domestic companies or each other, as licensees or licensors. In most countries the market shares not controlled by the transnationals are attributable to one or two large domestic companies, with only a very small percentage accounted for by smaller local companies. These large domestic companies have success with their own repertoire as well as licensing the transnationals. It is this 'symbiotic relationship' (Hellman, 1985) that ensures the transnationals' substantial oligopoly over the market for prerecorded music. Subsequently, it is also these successful domestic companies that the transnationals have been buying up.

Sales figures released show that the transnationals have tightened their grip on the European market (Burnett, 1992). The Big Six had the following total market shares (per cent) in 1990: Austria (94), France (83), Germany (87), Greece (70), Ireland (92), Italy (83), Netherlands (75), Portugal (89), Switzerland (93) and the UK (84). For the first half of 1991 the Big Six had the following pan-European chart shares (per cent) for albums: Polygram (21.2), Warner (20.5), EMI (27.9), BMG (12.5), Sony (11.3) and Others (6.6). The figures in the singles market were as follows:

EMI (27.2), Polygram (17.6), Warner (15.0), BMG (12.9), Sony (11.7) and Others (15.6). In terms of chart share it is significant to note that independent companies manage to do much better in the singles market than in the sales of albums.

A SUMMARY OF TRENDS

In a study partially concerned with the international music industry in 1977–8, Shore (1983) found that six transnational music corporations controlled between 50 and 100 per cent of record sales in the countries where they operated. While at first glance this would seem to confirm theories of dependency, Shore points out that a simple model of 'cultural imperialism' is not adequate to describe the character of their operations since these companies become involved in the production, manufacture and distribution of indigenous musics in addition to exporting music from their home countries. Shore goes on to argue that: 'The power and control of the music industry is ... better understood in terms of the co-optation and absorption of new music than in terms of a model that suggests the direct control and manipulation of public tastes' (Shore, 1983: 122).

A major motivating factor in consolidation and concentration of the music industry is distribution. Into the 1970s, the record industry relied in large measure on a series of independent record distributors that acted as intermediaries between the record manufacturers and retailers. In the 1980s the independent distribution system began to break down as more and more minor and independent labels such as Arista, Motown and A&M left independent distribution and agreed to be distributed by one of the major distributors. This consolidation trend has continued in recent years, and now many otherwise independent labels are distributed by one of the six transnationals.

Simultaneous with the consolidation of the music business within the transnationals has been a movement within those six phonogram companies to create numerous and varied satellite or auxiliary labels that will develop new talent and feed the enormous worldwide distribution networks they have established. So the two trends have been towards either the purchase of minor and independent labels by conglomerates, or the funding and distribution of start-up companies. Nevertheless, small independent companies continue to utilize independent distribution in segments of music that have specialized markets or niches.

In an article in the *New York Times*, music critic Jon Pareles noted that: 'As the record business enters the 1990s it has developed a two-tiered system. Independent labels handle specialized styles and new performers – they have almost taken over scouting for talent and test marketing it – while the majors grab proven contenders' (Pareles, 1990: 3). This concentration on consolidation leads to the search for huge 'mega' hits rather than broad profitability from various projects with a wide range of artists and musical styles. The huge hits almost inevitably come from a small group of international pop stars (who total less than 100), all of whom receive massive industry support and promotion commensurate with their sales histories and projected sales potentials. Today there are fewer artists signed to the major labels, fewer recordings released and fewer artists given a big promotional push than there were in the mid-1980s. Add to the picture the fact that the layoffs in the music industry in the period 1991 to 1993 were the deepest since the early 1980s and we begin to see how uncertainty is a constant factor to be dealt with.

The very general picture that emerges of the transnational music industry and the flow of phonograms described above is, certainly, not a simple one-way street. Popular music as communication is far more complex than is usually assumed. There are flows within flows and patterns of distribution that do not fit into the familiar simplistic model that implies domination. The phonogram industry is today important enough to be under the continual observation by cultural commissions and economic boards in various different nation states. In its 1989 report on the phono-gram industry, the Swedish cultural commission concluded that:

> the phonogram industry generally is in a stage of expansion and in Sweden as well as internationally can be described as an economically stable branch. Sales statistics point steadily upwards after a few prob-lematic years in the early 80s. The turning point coincided with the introduction of the CD to the marketplace. Consumer interest in phono-grams increased. The increased sales are mostly a matter of a relatively small number of titles sold in very large numbers. A similar pattern is to be found in other culture industries.
>
> (Statens Kulturråd, 1989, my translation)

What are these similar patterns to be found in other culture industries? How are we to understand the transition apparently simultaneously taking place in several different industries? What are the factors behind these changes and what are the consequences they can have? These questions and more are the type we shall take up and examine in the remaining chapters. In doing so we must limit the investigation to the transnational phonogram companies and their struggle for world dominance. We will also be mostly concerned with the marketplace in the USA, as it is the largest and most important, but will delve into other markets, such as Sweden, too, when examining recent industry trends. In proceeding, we must first establish our categories of description as well as our explanatory model. This will be done in the following chapters.

Chapter 5

The production of popular music

Market segmentation, distribution, brand loyalty, new product launches ... the industry fits quite neatly into the consumer goods category – especially if it is looked at from the top down.

(music company executive)

SYSTEMS ANALYSIS

Some of the most promising research developments in the study of the production and consumption of popular culture have been the attempts to use the tools of industrial and organizational sociology (see Lewis, 1978). This research attempts to answer the following types of questions. What sort of constraints do systems of production and consumption place upon one another? How do these systems affect the content and reception of popular culture? What is the relationship between culture industries and the larger societal institutions? This focus on 'culture industries' serves as a timely reminder that the mass media are first and foremost work organizations that depend upon the labour of workers, technicians, engineers and managers at a variety of levels of skill. This fact is often submerged below the otherwise exciting self-image the media projects of itself in various forms of 'infotainment'.

DiMaggio and Hirsch (1976) have delineated three major organizational approaches to popular culture production, ranging from closed to open systems, or from micro to macro levels. The first of these approaches focuses on the individual and his/her occupational role or career in inter-action with the popular culture organization. The studies of gatekeepers, occupational socialization and creators versus institutional constraints are typical subjects for attention.

The second type of research takes the culture organization as a whole, and its administration, as the focus of analysis, and hence examines production requirements and coordination tasks. The third approach is

inter-organizational or institutional analysis, which examines the relationship between culture industries and the larger societal environment.
Ownership of the media, constraints on the industry, market structure and
the role of technology exemplify this approach.

In studying the transnational music industry the most useful approach
is the third, open or macro systems, model which focuses on the cultural,
economic, technological and political factors or constraints in which culture
industries act as a major institution. At the same time we can comple-
ment the open systems approach with common elements from the closed
and semi-open approaches as Hirsch (1978) suggests, in order to take
advantage of all the available information.

THE PRODUCTION OF CULTURE PERSPECTIVE

Cultural production occurs within and is shaped by what Paul DiMaggio
(1977) calls the 'cultural economy'. It is hoped that by examining the ways
in which the activities of culture-producing organizations such as the
transnational music corporations shape cultural products, we can gain
insight into the process whereby culture is produced, distributed and
consumed in modern industrial society. In other words we can increase
our understanding of the 'cultural economy'.

A dominant theme in the social science study of the culture/society relationship has been the notion that culture reflects social structure, and that
cultural symbols (music, art, literature, movies, science) can be used for
uncovering the characteristics of social structure (see Peterson, 1979;
Rosengren, 1985; McQuail, 1987). Within this tradition, researchers have
tried to locate the basic value structure of society within the symbols it
produces. Studies into the sociology of popular culture have sought to
understand values through popular songs, television programmes, films
and literature, etc. Implicit in this view is, first, that culture creators
produce symbols reflecting their basic values, and, second, that audiences
select from a wide variety of culture products those that are most consis-
tent with their world view (see Ryan, 1985). In most social science research
into popular culture, world view is seen to be determined by social
structure. In other words, the assumption is often made that by analysing
the content of these cultural product selections, the world view of both
the culture creator and culture consumer can be revealed.

An alternative approach to analysing the relationship between cultural
production, consumption and value structure has emerged since Peterson
(1976: 10) argued for a focus on organizational structures and production
processes by which the 'creation, manufacture, marketing, distribution,

exhibiting, inculcation, evaluation, and consumption' of cultural symbol systems are produced. From what has come to be known as a 'production of culture' perspective (Peterson, 1976), numerous scholars have pointed out that the constraints or contingencies within the cultural production process limit the range of products available at any given point in time.

If product choices are limited, consumers may withdraw from the marketplace and cease consumption, or, as is more often the case, make the best available choice from the limited range of products offered (Beebe, 1977; Ryan, 1985). This would indicate that audience choice alone is not necessarily the best indicator of value structure. In order to effectively evaluate the relationship between audience taste and values, one needs to determine the influence of culture-producing firms on the range of cultural products available.

Peterson's (1976) original vision of a sociology of cultural production set aside the idealist–materialist debate (whether culture creates social structure or vice versa) to study the production and reproduction of culture (see Ettema *et al.*, 1987: 748). Such a perspective is not without its critics. Tuchman (1983: 332), for example, argues that most production of culture research is simply another brand of organizational sociology that doesn't question modern capitalism and thus obscures 'the historicity of cultural products' and how these products are 'implicated in the creation of ideology'. Tuchman stresses the importance of focusing on the reproduction of ideology during the production process.

Writing from a different perspective, Jensen (1984: 110) claims that the production of culture perspective neglects the fact that cultural production encompasses 'both the producers and the audience for which they create'. For Jensen the crucial point to be made is that: 'Culture is not defined as a container of messages processed along a line from sender to receiver, but as the means through which people construct meaningful worlds in which to live' (Jensen, 1984: 108).

The critiques forwarded by both Tuchman and Jensen are both valid and very relevant but, at the same time, if we are to discuss the consumption of music and the making sense or meaning out of that music we must first consider how the production of commodities is at the same time a preselection of possibilities. By not exploring the production processes one cannot explain the limits within which people are free to make their own sense or pleasure out of popular music.

In emphasizing the process of culture creation and dissemination, the production of culture perspective can well help us to better understand the possible ways in which social structure possibly influences culture.

As Peterson (1976) has argued, the best way to reveal the relationship between society and culture is by 'turning from the global corpus of habitual culture and focusing instead on the processes by which elements of culture are fabricated in those milieux where symbol-system production is most self-consciously the center of activity' (Peterson, 1976: 10).

The production of culture perspective has, to date, produced a wide variety of cultural industry research. For example, Peterson (1982, 1985) has studied the emergence of rock 'n' roll in the 1950s, and the production of literary works. Cantor (1980) examined television production, while Becker (1982) has studied art production. The book publishing industry has been studied by Coser *et al.* (1982), while Ryan (1985) focused on the music publishing business.

Peterson (1982, 1985) isolates six factors or constraints that alone, or in combination, often facilitate cultural production. These constraints include: technology, law, industry structure, organizational structure, the market and occupational careers. These six constraints typically influence the cultural world in interaction with each other and as such it should not be misconstrued that technology, law, etc., are simply imposed from outside. It must be fully recognized that various interest groups within the world of the 'cultural economy' actively support or compete with each other to shape, implement or oppose the influence of one constraint on another. The biggest problem with Peterson's six constraints is that they can be considered rather random and are really on different levels of abstraction that perhaps have little to do with each other. It would be a mistake to interpret the constraints too rigidly and attempt to apply them in a slavish manner.

In order to bring together theoretical arguments and to provide a necessary framework for their development, a production of culture model can be outlined as follows. The essential components of the production of culture model are the six constraints or factors summarized by Peterson (1985), namely:

1 *Technology*. This refers to all the technologies that are involved in the production and manufacturing of cultural products as well as those involved in the eventual dissemination and reception of such.
2 *Law*. Laws and administrative codes shape the financial and aesthetic conditions within which cultural production can develop. Copyright law is particularly important in that it transforms whole classes of creative activity into private property that can be bought, sold and stolen like any other goods. Laws can shape the development of whole art forms.

3   *Market.* The market refers to the audience as it is identified and conceptualized by financial decision makers within a culture industry. The market is what is considered when firms decide if the profit margin realized will justify the production, distribution and promotion of a cultural product. The ways in which the producers view the audience directly influences what will be produced.

4   *Industry structure.* The structure of the industry has to do with the number and relative size of firms in the market producing cultural products.

5   *Organizational structure.* The structure of culture-producing companies varies according to their size. As the firm size increases and jobs become more specialized, records, books, etc., are increasingly viewed as products and are shaped to fit a standardized 'product image'.

6   *Occupational careers.* The ways creative people define their occupations and organize their careers can greatly influence the nature of the work they produce. Career denotes a somewhat predictable sequence of positions through which a person normally moves in the course of an occupation.

It must be stressed that these six components rarely act in isolation but in fact are always in interaction with an exogenous variable, the social world as represented by the social, economic, political and environmental context of society. These six constraints when used in concert have generated a number of hypotheses relating to the production of culture. Perhaps the most powerful and certainly one of the most controversial of these hypotheses is about the relationship between the number of competing firms in a market and the corresponding level of product diversity. This is known as the concentration and diversity debate. Before we turn our attention to this debate we must first further develop our systems model.

LOOSELY COUPLED SYSTEMS MODEL

As mentioned above, two major themes in the sociology of culture are the production and consumption of culture. Students of the former study the institutions, processes, politics and economics of the production of ideas, often embodied in products such as art, music, literature, radio, television, film and other aesthetic domains. Students of the latter examine patterns of cultural choice, looking at how individuals spend their time and money on various leisure-time activities, including sports, watching television and film, reading and listening to music of various kinds.

These traditions come together in the production of culture work that emphasizes the relationship between concentration among the producers of cultural products and the diversity of the cultural product. The relationships between these variables and their explanations are of wide interest and may well characterize the production and consumption of culture generally.

In order to better grasp these theoretical notions we will see in the following sections that there exist largely separate complex systems for the production and consumption of popular music. The observed relationships between changes in concentration and diversity reflect connections between two loosely coupled systems. 'Loosely coupled' refers to systems in which interactions within subsystems are substantially stronger than interactions between subsystems. (See, for example, Simon, 1981; Simon and Ando, 1961; Fisher, 1961; Brunner and Brewer, 1971; Glassman, 1973; March and Olsen, 1976; Weick, 1976; Meyer and Rowan, 1978; Ouchi, 1978; Perrow, 1986.)

Simon (1981: 209) refers to these as 'nearly decomposable systems':

Hierarchic systems are ... often nearly decomposable. Hence only aggregate properties of their parts enter into the description of the interactions of those parts. A generalization of the notion of near decomposability might be called the 'empty world hypothesis' – most things are only weakly connected with most other things; for a tolerable description of reality only a tiny fraction of all possible interactions needs to be taken into account.

(Simon, 1981: 221)

The highly complex system for the production of (musical) culture – the firms, roles, structures and processes – are analytically, if not factually, distinct from the system of cultural consumption. In effect, the connections and ties *within* these systems are substantially stronger than the connections and ties *between* them. The relations among record producers, artists, marketing and promotion specialists, trade press and so on, are stronger than the relationships between producers and consumers. As elaborated below, consumers, largely teenagers and young adults, interact among themselves and with mass media, including radio, television and film. Opinion leaders may take into account various fan and music review publications. Weak as these latter ties are, the mainly separate systems of production and consumption are connected through the media, concerts and an economic act: the purchase of phonograms. In the model, the aggregate behaviour of each system is such that it weakly influences the behaviour of the other.

Consumers indicate their choices through purchases and changes in preference behaviour. Peer group interaction combined with the influence of media and advertising campaigns may shift purchases from one musical fad or trend to another. As detailed below, it is suggested that cohort succession combined with adolescent differentiation and rebellion are major factors that drive this change in musical tastes. Also, to the extent that new directions in popular music are innovated by smaller, independent producers, the increasing diversity of musical products has led historically to the decline in concentration of Top 10 hits among the leading producer firms. However, because of vertical and horizontal integration, the major producers are now more unlikely to lose their control of the market while musical diversity will fluctuate more widely, reflecting changes on the demand side – specifically, changes in musical taste and fashion.

Figure 5.1 summarizes the reconceptualization of the production and consumption of popular music as a loosely coupled systems model. The model includes the *production system* (aesthetic and material) and the *consumption system*. The links and connections *within* both aesthetic and material production are characterized as being strong. The links *between* aesthetic and material production are also characterized as strong. The consumption system consists of a series of weak links and connections. The links *between* the system of production and consumption are also characterized as weak. The model is by no means exclusive or complete but is meant simply as a heuristic tool to illustrate the mainly separate systems of production and consumption and how they relate to one another. The list of component parts to each system could be made to go on almost indefinitely but has instead been shortened to include only the most relevant parts. We can now discuss each system separately.

PRODUCTION SYSTEM

The production system includes the artists who transform ideas into popular culture artifacts, and all the people who develop the artifacts from original form into marketable items. Agents, producers, managers and executives are active here in making decisions about which to market, how to package, and how much money to spend on developing, promoting and distributing. In the realms of popular culture, for example,

Each object must be 'discovered', sponsored, and brought to public attention by entrepreneurial organizations or nonprofit agencies before

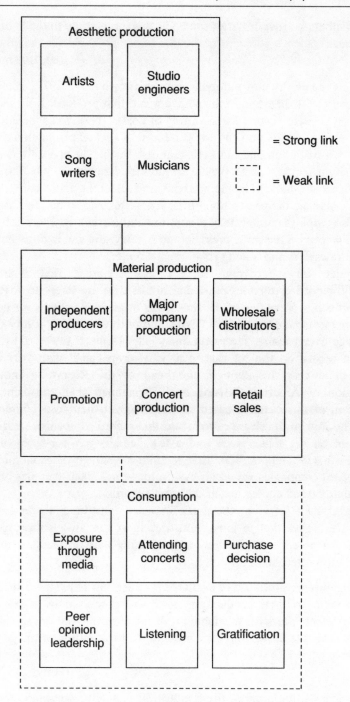

Figure 5.1 Production and consumption systems of popular music

the originating artist or writer can be linked successfully to the intended audience.

(Hirsch, 1972: 640)

In studying the production of popular culture, Hirsch (1972, 1977), Peterson and Berger (1971, 1975) and others have noted that producer firms evolve specialized roles to accomplish a variety of goals. These goals include the identification of artists and cultural products, the actual production of the record, its distribution and marketing, and so forth. The specialized roles include talent scouts, agents, producers, and the like, whose job is to contract with artists, make judgements about, and select the actual songs to be recorded, manage the production of the recording, and so on. The organization also employs specialists in promotion and marketing whose job is to promote records in the trade press, on radio, television and in films, among record wholesalers and among retail record outlets.

Dependent on a particular scarce resource, namely, that of artistic creativity, record companies must find artists who are likely to write or record hit songs. Very few of the thousands of aspiring artists ever get so far as a recording contract (Frith, 1981), and of those that do, a very small percentage ever become successful financially. Denisoff (1975: 92) likens getting a record on the hit lists to a 'vinyl crap game' with very little chance of success. In addition, the head of the Recording Industry Association of America (RIAA) in 1979 claimed that approximately 80 per cent of all records released failed to recover their costs (*Billboard*, 1979). This low hit to release ratio means that record companies are highly dependent on big sellers such that a few winners pay for most of the losers. Frith (1981) points out that to take advantage of economies of scale, record companies would always prefer to sell 500,000 copies of one record than 50,000 copies of ten different records.

In Hirsch's (1970) view, the music industry constitutes a preselection system. He argues that in most industries there are always more goods available for possible production and marketing than are actually manufactured, promoted and consumed.

More goods are produced or available than actually reach the consumer. Subsequent to their production, these are processed by a selection system which filters the available products, ensuring that only a sample of the available universe is ever brought to the attention of the general public.

(Hirsch, 1970: 5)

Hirsch suggests that none of these industries is able to accurately predict which of the items produced will pass successfully through each stage of the complex filter to allow for the production and promotion of only those items likely to succeed. Record companies can predict success reasonably well with an established star, but not so well for new artists.

The organizations competing in the market for record sales evolved these specialized roles, structures and processes in order to maximize their profits, actual or potential, and to minimize their risks. Since the producers of popular music are largely at the mercy of shifting tastes and fads (see Hirsch, 1972), the producing organizations try to minimize their financial exposure, for example, by signing only a few of the very successful artists to long-term contracts, preferring instead to deal with most artists on a short-term basis. Because of the risks associated with the market, producers try to hedge their bets by overproducing within musical genres and by producing diverse cultural products. Record producers are motivated to overproduce by the expectation that at least a few of their records will be big sellers and return more than enough profit to cover the costs of the more numerous low-selling records.

The main coping strategy of the music industry is that of overproduction and differential promotion of new items. In practice, this means producing a large number of items (album titles) and promoting only a select few or those that seem to be catching on. The hope is that at least some of the products will be accepted by distributors, retailers and, finally, the public. Denisoff (1975) called this the 'buckshot theory of record releasing'. The use of the overproduction strategy can have both positive and negative implications for new recording artists. In order to have a full roster of musical styles, firms look for new artists. The downside is that new artists almost never get the kind of publicity and marketing support they need to gain the notice of distributors, retailers, the media and the public.

In the past and often simultaneously with overproduction, record companies have employed three other strategies to maximize sales and profits. First, leading firms usually produce records in a variety of styles. Some are intended to compete directly with songs and artists already high on the charts, so-called 'cover' records. Second, firms sometimes produce records by their own artists that have a similar 'sound' to leading performers. Third, firms may record innovative acts in the hope that they will start a new trend or fad.

Traditionally, the artist and repertoire (A&R) department has had the responsibility to find new talent and to see that the artist is recorded to best advantage (Vogel, 1986: 145). The A&R person works closely with the artist and the record producer to ensure that the recording sessions go well and that the final sound mix satisfies the company, the artist and, hopefully, the public. However, Ryan and Peterson (1982) show at the various stages of writing, publishing and recording popular music, decision-makers work from a product image geared more towards satisfying decision-makers at the next stage of production than satisfying the final consuming audience. Like other formal organizations, culture-production firms tend towards bureaucratic or instrumental rationalism.

In the recording business, the emphasis on marketing has resulted in developing what is called a product-image orientation towards songs (Ryan and Peterson, 1982). Songs are referred to by words indicating the stage in the decision process through which the song passes: 'property', 'copyright', 'demo', 'tape', 'cut', 'master', 'release', 'product' and, finally, a 'hit' or a 'dud'. That sort of product-image language focuses the attention of the creative people on the commercial rather than the artistic values of the work; it also increases the power of the marketing and promotion departments. Indeed, in a typical recording company, the most influential departments have marketing, promotion or sales responsibilities.

The big-hit emphasis has a far-reaching impact on song writers (ibid., 1982). Frequently, composers must take into account the product image that a recording company is attempting to portray for its recordings. Indeed, some successful song writers have developed what is termed a 'commercial professional strategy' based on an image of what will be accepted by music publishers and others down the decision chain in the production and marketing processes.

More recently, the record producer function has been increasingly taken over by freelance producers and sound engineers (Kealy, 1982: 104). Most producers today are independent and often work only in their own recording studios or studios where they have special business arrangements rather than in studios owned by the major producers. Although the company-employed studio engineer was a conservative force aesthetically in the past, since the 1960s the sound mixer has been increasingly at the forefront of aesthetic changes in popular music. They are responsible for what Kealy (ibid.) calls the 'real rock revolution'. George Martin, the so-called 'fifth Beatle', is a prime example. Today's hot producers like David Foster, Brian Eno, Daniel Lanois or Steve Lillywhite command enormous salaries and are generally booked up years in advance.

Once a master tape is produced, the final studio sound mix is sent to the factory for mass production. The actual manufacturing and distribution of records are costly processes (Vogel, 1986: 146) where economies of scale and capital resources benefit the major producers. Consequently, at various times in the history of the recording industry, vertical integration

and the resulting economies have made it difficult for smaller, independent producers to compete in the marketplace.

Before a record is ready for distribution, the record company typically
evolves a marketing and promotion plan, with the 'project team' deciding
where and in what quantities to distribute a record and how to market
the record to its target audience (Negus, 1992). The distributors get records
to the retailers and to the subdistributors such as 'rackjobbers' who service
the shelves in retail outlets, for example, in department stores and super-
markets (Baskerville, 1979: 248). The major producers have consolidated
their hold on distribution channels. Thus, the 1980s saw a change from
retail sales via well-stocked music shops with knowledgeable staff to rack
sales via small outlets lacking knowledgeable staff and a trend towards a
few large record or 'mega' stores, especially in major cities.

The organizational structure of recording companies varies according
to their size. In a small company the relationship towards the recording artist can easily be intimate, long lasting and constructive in the long,
complex process of releasing a record (Denisoff, 1975). As the firm size
increases and jobs become more specialized, records are increasingly
viewed as products and shaped to fit a standardized product image (Ryan
and Peterson, 1982).

The phonogram industry can be divided into three major segments:
manufacturing, distributing and retailing. The manufacturing category
includes master producers, recording studios and pressing plants. The
distributing category includes wholesale distributors, sub-distributors and
rackjobbers. The remaining category includes stores and record clubs.
Within the industry, major firms are integrated both vertically and hori-
zontally to different degrees. At the organizational level a noticeable move
towards integration took place in the late 1980s. This integration has taken
place with the majors striving to gather as many functions as possible
under their corporate umbrella in order to rationalize their costs.

Competition between phonogram manufacturers is mostly in the form
of product differentiation, which is an important factor in an oligopolistic
industry. Phonogram companies manufacture products under different
labels. The manufacturer usually owns several labels and distributes
several others. Changes occur as labels are discontinued and others added
or merged between companies. Each phonogram company seeks to maximize its market share by promoting recordings through advertising, radio
play, music television and other forms of publicity. A critical key to success
in the phonogram industry is the ability to discover and develop new
talent. Today, as the number of records produced by independent
producers has increased, the transnationals have been quite satisfied to

manufacture, distribute and promote independent records by securing them through licensing arrangements.

At the distribution level, competition is generally more service oriented than price oriented. The main variation in prices paid by retailers to distributors occurs because subdistributors (small volume) charge higher rates than do regular distributors (large volume). The main form of price competition in the phonogram industry occurs at the retail level. As the number of retail outlets grows there can be considerable variation from one store to another in the price charged for the same product (Vogel, 1986).

As stated earlier, the transnational phonogram companies have traditionally worked in two basic ways. In most countries they have their own fully owned subsidiaries, or else they have a joint partnership with a local company. These subsidiary companies perform all the functions that are performed by local companies and in most countries in which they operate they tend to dominate the market. In the countries where the transnationals do not have subsidiaries, they usually have a licensee who manufactures and/or distributes their product.

Licensing arrangements are in many ways one of the central mechanisms for the flow of music internationally. Licensing deals generally work the same way in all countries regardless of who is the licensee or licensor. Foreign licensees pay a basic royalty rate to the licensor (label of origin) based upon the retail list price in the original country of manufacture or sale (Shemel and Krasilovsky, 1979). The licensee always pays an advance on royalties. This guarantees the licensor with an immediate cash flow. It also means that the licensee will actively promote sales of the record to recoup the investment. Almost all licensing contracts require that the licensee release an agreed upon minimum number of records for the duration of the agreement.

The licensor does not send the finished product (phonograms), but sends a copy of the master tape, which is the final recording studio mix. The licensee, or most often the transnational subsidiary, uses the master tape to manufacture records locally. Once the CDs have been manufactured (pressed and packaged), the local licensee, or subsidiary, performs all the usual functions including marketing, distribution and promotion in attempting to make the song a hit. If the licensee does not have the capacity to manufacture, distribute or promote the phonograms it will subcontract these functions out to yet another company or companies.

There are two main reasons why phonograms are manufactured locally. It is less expensive to manufacture locally than to transport bulk phonograms from country to country. By manufacturing locally companies can avoid paying heavy import duties and taxes that apply to finished products (phonograms). There are situations, however, where phonograms are not manufactured locally but imported into a country as a finished product. This occurs when there is a lack of sufficient local manufacturing facilities and capacity. For example, Sweden continues to import a major portion of all phonograms sold. In the countries where the transnationals and their subsidiaries operate their own manufacturing facilities they require constant work to maintain their economies of scale. Therefore, in Europe for example, many of the transnationals find it cost efficient to centralize their manufacturing to one plant and then distribute from there by freight truck. Short road distances and European Common Market agreements make this unproblematic. Sony and Polygram generally manufacture most of their phonograms in The Netherlands, while Warner and BMG concentrate their manufacturing in Germany for the European market. These phonograms are then distributed across the whole of Europe.

In the instances when the licensee manufactures the phonograms locally, the licensor generally provides all the items necessary for local release. This usually includes a copy of the master tape, picture negatives and art work for the album covers and liner notes. Licensors also send promotional materials to be used in advertising campaigns. These generally include suggestions for the ad campaign, biographical information on the artists, pictures and posters for retail displays. Music videos have increasingly become part of these promotional packages, as have prerecorded interviews with the artists.

ECOLOGICAL THEORY AND MUSIC INDUSTRY COMPETITION

Certain work in organizational ecology (Freeman, 1983; Carroll, 1984) is very useful in understanding the relationship between organizations in the contemporary media industry. Borrowing from biology we know that the way in which a population 'fits' into an ecosystem is called its 'ecological niche'. The term 'fundamental niche' refers to the resources a population is theoretically capable of using under ideal circumstances. The resources a population actually uses are collectively called its 'realized niche'. The 'competitive exclusion principle' states that two species cannot coexist in a community if their niches are identical. However, ecologically similar species can coexist in a community if there are one or more significant differences in their niches. This leads to 'resource partitioning', in which sympartic species consume slightly different foods or use other resources in slightly different ways.

Ecological theory is also concerned with 'symbiosis' (living together) which is a term that encompasses a variety of interactions in which two different species, a host and its symbiont, maintain a close association. There are three types of symbiotic interactions. In parasitism, one organism, the parasite, harms the host. In commensalism, one partner benefits without significantly affecting the other. In mutualism, both partners benefit from the relationship.

Let us now draw the analogy with the phonogram industry. According to the structure-within-industry branch analysis approach suggested by Porter (1980) and the ecological analysis of competition, suggested by Carroll (1985) and by Dimmick and Rothenbuhler (1984), one can examine how companies belonging to different strategic groups can turn out to be successful in competition. Most contemporary cultural industries are structurally divided into two strategic groups. The first group are the industry leaders (generalists), the major large companies that dominate the production, distribution, as well as the marketplace. The second group (specialists) are the various independent companies or industry minors which are a heterogeneous group of smaller firms and entrepreneurs. This dual structure enables one to distinguish between an industry 'core' and an industry 'periphery'.

The major companies (*generalists*) often provide mass products for a mass audience or a wide range of products for different groups of consumers. The minor companies (*specialists*) may concentrate on a limited product or genre. Thus the *generalist core* and the *specialist periphery* operate as two distinctly different strategic groups within an industry. Firms within the generalist group resemble each other closely and are likely to respond in a similar fashion to market disturbances. Specialist firms tend to be somewhat more heterogeneous.

According to ecological theory one can consider the media industry as a population; a company as a member or organism of this population, and audiences, and cultural products, as resources necessarily required for the healthy maintenance of the population.

Competition among companies is a component of 'industry ecology'. The main concept of this theory is the 'niche'. The concept of niche refers to a distinct combination of resources that can support organizations with similar goals, boundaries and activities. Generally, when one production firm perceives a niche, attempts to exploit it, and thrives, other firms enter to compete in the niche (Hannan and Freeman, 1988).

The 'niche breadth' is a measure of the area of a niche. In media industries, niche can be seen as having three dimensions, consisting of types of capital, types of audience and types of content. 'Niche overlap' refers to the area of niche space shared by adjacent niches. In competition, populations with highly similar resource utilization will overlap strongly, thus displaying a high ecological similarity. Niche overlap is thus a measure of competition between companies.

According to Dimmick and Rothenbuhler (1984) and Carroll (1985), companies within an industry tend to create a resource usage pattern (niche), ideal to its environment. The major companies, the industry core, tend to compete in a number of domains simultaneously, aiming at a broad niche and displaying a 'generalist' strategy. The minor firms, the industry periphery, typically utilize fewer resources and a 'specialist' strategy. These are of course theoretical ideal types and in reality firms operate somewhere between generalism and specialism.

As Carroll (1985: 1266) explains, organizations

> differ in niche width. An ecological niche is defined as the n-dimensional resource space within which a population can exist. Populations that depend on a wide range of environmental resources for survival are known as generalists. Organizational generalists . . . can operate in almost any environment because they average outcomes across a wide range of conditions. In contrast populations that survive in a specific environmental condition (or within a narrow range of environmental resources) are called specialists.

From this perspective, the relationship between industry concentration and diversity can be explained by what Carroll (1985) also calls the 'resource partitioning model' in which the producers and consumers (the resources) are divided (partitioned) between generalist and specialist firms. As concentration increases and as the large, generalist firms produce more homogeneous products, they create opportunities for more innovative and specialized firms whose products appeal to more narrow markets. However, as their products gain marketshares, these specialized firms are absorbed by larger firms, thereby increasing concentration and again creating new opportunities for smaller firms. This view has been applied to culture-producing organizations such as newspapers (Carroll, 1985), book publishers (Powell, 1985), the music industry (Burnett, 1990a) and video producers (Hellman and Soramäki, 1994).

The phonogram industry provides a good example of niche overlap. The six transnationals compete, basically, with each other for the same audience and with similar products. The transnationals or generalist firms have shared the mass audience mainstream media music market between them, with the resulting niche overlap functioning as the status quo in the industry and thus acting as an entry barrier against newcomers.

As noted above, mature industries are dominated by generalist organizations that represent the equilibrium state of a long competitive process dictated by economies of scale. In their competition for audiences and marketshare, firms in the media industry differentiate their products from their principal competitors to avoid niche overlap. The phonogram companies do this through their differing roster of musical artists, a form of resource partitioning.

The dualistic approach outlined above raises certain questions about middle-size or middle-tier companies. Typically, they are part of the oligopolistic sector, the industry core, but when competition for market share hardens they are often the prey for takeover attempts by the industry leaders. As has been noted above, in the music industry the middle-size firms have proven to be vulnerable to takeover attempts and have essentially disappeared from the international scene. This would seem to suggest that as the generalist market concentrates it leaves more available audience resources for specialist firms, thus enhancing their life expectancy (Carroll, 1985).

In summary, the ecological theory of competition suggests that differentiation and specialization are the main competitive strategies which result in the dual structure, a difference between generalists and specialists. Several analyses concerning the phonogram industry have revealed this new division of labour, one of mutual interdependence or symbiosis, between the major and independent companies. There is abundant empirical evidence that the independent or alternative labels experiment with sounds, trends and artists, thus serving as a test market for the entire industry. The major companies use this information and in turn offer their manufacturing, marketing and distribution services to the smaller companies (e.g. Burnett, 1990a, 1992b; Lopes, 1992; Frith, 1988b; Hellman, 1983).

Under current conditions of oligopoly, one can say that independent labels have their own rather specialized niche within the music industry. The number of independent firms producing 'music from the fringe' has shown signs of increasing in recent years. This would seem to support the ecological resource partitioning model according to which concentration of the generalist market segment leaves more room for specialist operations.

Chapter 6

The consumption of popular music

If music be the food of love, play on.
(Shakespeare, *Twelfth Night*, I.i.1)

THE CONSUMPTION SYSTEM

The consumption of popular music is equally complex and also comprises in itself an entire system that includes consumers and gatekeepers (see Figure 5.1). The latter include radio stations, television, films, advertising, newspapers, the music press, etc. The efforts of the producer firms are mediated by these various 'gatekeepers' (Hirsch, 1977), especially mass media. Gatekeepers are the people who make key decisions about whether or not to select certain materials for production and distribution. Traditionally, radio stations have been the most important gatekeepers: the output of the record industry is the input of the radio industry. Since the goal of commercial radio is profit and since the source of profit is the difference between programme costs and advertising revenues, a symbiotic relationship has developed between radio stations and record companies. Playing music on the radio usually entails significantly less production costs than other types of programming.

Music producers are equally reliant on radio stations to get their recordings exposed to the buying public. Competition for air-time is extremely high. Most popular music stations add three or four new songs to their play list each week. Compared to the approximately 7,000 singles and up to 5,000 albums, each with some 10 songs per album, that are released each year, this indicates just how difficult it is to get a song presented to the public (Vogel, 1986: 148).

While radio has been central to promoting records in the past, music television and movies increasingly play a more important role in bringing new artists and records to the attention of phonogram consumers (Burnett, 1987). For example, as early as 1983 a Nielsen study in the USA (cited in *Variety*, 1983) claimed that MTV (music television) was more influential than radio in the record-buying behaviour of 12 to 34 year olds. Similarly, Roe and Löfgren(1988) found that music television was a more important source of information about popular music than radio in Swedish cable households.

The importance of the mass media gatekeepers should not be underestimated for they make the 'key' decisions and the public's own options are limited by these decisions as people can only 'want' from amongst what they can get. As Hirsch (1970: 66) observes, the preselection system has built-in feedback mechanisms. These feedback mechanisms include the weak links in Figure 5.1. The most important of these is the purchase decision/sales link that connects producers and consumers via an economic act.

The market refers to the audience as it is identified and conceptualized by financial decision makers within the popular culture industry. The market is what is considered when firms decide if the profit margin realized will justify the production, distribution and promotion of a record. The ways in which the transnationals view the audience directly influences what will be produced. Peterson has shown how the terms 'formula', 'convention', 'audience image' and 'product image' have been used by researchers to suggest how artistic and financial decision makers redefine the heterogeneous and unknown mass of potential consumers as a homogeneous and predictable market that can be exploited (Peterson, 1985).

In the 1990s the transnationals appear to be increasingly concentrating on a mass homogeneous market image. One important effect is the emphasis on 'blockbuster tie-ins', which is an essentially conservative strategy designed to minimize the risks of production in an unstable market. These records are designed as cross-media products which can be advertised and promoted in a systematic way. Tie-ins between books, films and records are liked because the success of one product contributes to the appeal of the others. The book/movie/hit song tie-in is so pervasive that during the summer of 1986 there were seven different movie theme songs in the American Top 40 charts (Burnett, 1987). Since then the number of movie-related hit songs has increased to the point where it is hard to imagine a hit movie without a hit song or soundtrack.

Movies and music have always enjoyed a certain amount of collaborative success, from early recordings of musicals and vaudeville shows right up to the phenomenal success of movie soundtrack albums such as *Saturday Night Fever*. In recent years these two industries have worked together on an unprecedented level, as filmmakers found that the use of diverse popular music in soundtracks could result in success for both the movie and the soundtrack album. Bryan Adams's single '(Everything I Do) I Do It For You' became one of the biggest selling singles in history partially because it was the theme song to the film *Robin Hood: Prince of Thieves* starring Kevin Costner. Likewise the soundtrack album to the film *The Bodyguard* featuring Whitney Houston and Kevin Costner became one of the largest selling albums of all time.

As noted above, the large entertainment conglomerates through a twin strategy of vertical and horizontal integration have extended their traditional operations into new markets. They see their new subsidiaries as vehicles to help smooth out the high and low earning periods that occur in the mass media industries. Today's entertainment conglomerates look at their various companies and alliances as parts of a package that should be utilized to enhance corporate strengths across the media. The music industry is increasingly integrated into the other leisure and cultural industries: one of the results being the new all pervasive cultural commodity – the rock video of the song of the movie of the book (see Goodwin, 1986).

The consumption system is also where the reception and use of popular music takes place and is the last stage in the communication process. Here one can also examine the role systems of the audience. How do they react to cultural artifacts? What do they demand? How does popular culture influence them? How do they group, demographically, and in terms of taste? Here is the 'space' where the variables such as age, gender, education, status, income, urbanization, peers and media habits can be of real use to the researcher.

Who are the consumers of popular music? A study (1990) in the United States conducted by the Recording Industry Association of America (RIAA) shows that in terms of total dollars spent on phonograms of all kinds, 10 to 14 year olds purchased 9 per cent of all music, 15 to 19 year olds 23 per cent, 20 to 24 year olds 22 per cent, 25 to 34 year olds 24 per cent, and the 35-plus group purchased 22 per cent of recorded music.

Music often becomes mainstream only after an earlier incarnation as a counterculture genre. Successive cohorts of adolescents approach their entry into adult society by adopting novel forms of music that set them apart from that very mainstream. Jazz, blues, rock 'n' roll, punk, rap and heavy metal were all at one time viewed by mainstream society as emblems of adolescent rebellion (Chaffee, 1985: 416). Gradually these music-based subcultures become incorporated into the mainstream as adherents of a particular musical wave grow older. Thus, a repetitive cycle of subcultural rebellion and innovation followed by gradual absorption into the popular music category manifests itself in new styles of music.

Marcuse (1964: 56) argues that an important characteristic of modern industrial societies based on instrumental rationalism is their ability to incorporate within the dominant culture ideas that have the potential to 'transcend' or 'negate' it. Thus, the incorporation or co-optation of successive waves of music largely based on themes of adolescent rebellion is an instance of this general process.

Denisoff and Levine (1970: 39) propose that 'Mannheim's notion of generational units in conflict can best be examined in terms of life styles and cultural leanings rather than conventional political ideologies'. Rock 'n' roll in the 1950s was perceived by adults as 'deviating from the outward symbols of respectability and the basic normative order' (ibid.: 40). In this sense, rock 'n' roll was a deviation advocating a temporary role suspension for youth, but not questioning basic values and institutions in society. In contrast, rock music in the 1960s questioned basic values and institutions, while urging social change. Whereas rock 'n' roll in the 1950s was seen as an expression of 'rebellious youth', rock in the 1960s was viewed by many adults as politically dissident and morally subversive and bankrupt. Thus, Denisoff and Levine conclude that different generational units perceive the ideology of popular music in very different ways.

Although repeated exposure to popular music through concerts, the media and listening to recorded music may lead to gratification, it may also lead to decreased gratification. When the available music is perceived to be of the same genre or aesthetic fad as previous music, gratification will decline since the ability of the listener to differentiate her/himself from preceding cohorts of popular music fans is also diminished.

Changes in cohort size may also affect popular culture. Rieger (1975) argues that the shrinking teenage cohort in the United States in the future will cause the teenage market to stagnate or decline. As they age, earlier cohorts will continue to listen to pop music, but at reduced rates. Still, the pop music audience will span a larger age range to include more middle-aged listeners. American Census Bureau projections of the size of the 5- to 24-year-old age group show that the relative size of this group will continue to decline into the next century, and that in absolute terms, the number of youth in this group in 1995 will be a million less than in 1985. Assuming no changes in the allocation of disposable income, these numbers suggest that at least the American market for new rock recordings peaked in the mid-1970s.

COPYRIGHT

When examining the culture industry, law and technology are often over-looked. Laws and administrative codes shape the financial and aesthetic conditions within which music can develop. Traditionally, music publishers acted as middlemen between composers and record companies and collected a mechanical royalty on behalf of the composer for every recording sold and a performance royalty for every time a musical piece was performed live or played on the radio. Today that situation has changed with the major music companies, through the strategy of vertical and horizontal integration, now controlling the major publishers. The consequences on the international level are enormous, as there has been a continued growth of copyright infringement. Wallis and Malm (1984) see the increasing problems of maintaining a functioning international copyright system where funds are exchanged between countries according to the usage of music as so serious that, 'the copyright system could collapse in a matter of years' (Wallis and Malm, 1984: 319).

Copyright exists in material which comes within one of the categories prescribed as being capable of having copyright protection. For our immediate concerns this area of work and subject matter is described as 'musical works' and 'sound recordings'. Copyright subsists for defined periods which differ according to the category of subject matter or work. If material is entitled to copyright, then the right vested in the copyright owner is that of preventing others from doing certain specified acts, called 'the restricted acts'. The restricted acts are specified by the Copyright Act in relation to each category of work and subject matter, and differ accordingly (Biederman et al., 1992).

For *musical works* the relevant restricted acts are as follows: reproducing the work in any material form; publishing the work; performing the work in public; broadcasting the work; causing the work to be transmitted to subscribers by a diffussion service; or making an adaptation. For *sound recordings* the relevant restricted acts are: making a record embodying the recording; causing the recording to be heard in public; or broadcasting the recording.

A successful song writer/musician will expect to derive income from a number of different sources all of which arise as a result of the law on copyright or 'intellectual property'. She will expect to receive royalties from the sale of sheet music, from the live performance of her work and also as a result of people making recordings of her work. A performer will also expect to receive royalties on the sale of her records and the playing of those records in public. Different organizations exist to keep track of the different incomes due. In the UK the main organizations are the Performing Right Society (PRS) and the Mechanical Copyright Protection Society Limited (MCPS). In the United States it is the American Society of Composers, Authors and Publishers (ASCAP) and Broadcast Music Incorporated (BMI). In Germany it is the Gesellschaft für Musikalische Aufführungs (GEMA) and in France the Société des Auteurs, Compositeurs et Editeurs de Musique (SACEM). In Sweden, the Svenska Tonsättares Internationella Musikbyrå (STIM) fulfils a similar function.

MUSIC PUBLISHING

The 'song' has always been and remains the focus of the music publishing industry. The creation, discovery, protection, licensing, exploitation and resulting income derived from songs has a great effect on how the industry is run on a day-to-day basis. The functions of the music publisher include working on a creative level with song writers in the composing of new songs, protecting and enforcing their copyrights, seeking potential licensees for songs, entering into licensing arrangements and collecting and distributing the resulting income. Just as the songs have changed, technology has changed the way in which music publishers do business, enlarged potential sources of income and made the industry much more complex. Virtually all the technological innovations affecting the entertainment industries in recent years, including cable and satellite television, videocassettes, compact discs and other digital formats have resulted in the expansion of the music publishing business through new outlets and greater usage of music. Music publishing now generates more than $3 billion of income per year worldwide, and unlike retail sales, is expanding.

The structure of the music publishing industry is similar to that of the recording industry in many ways and different in others. The similarity stems from the concentration that has occurred in recent years in virtually all of the entertainment industries. As the business became much more international in scope and as inflation dramatically drove up the cost of signing the next potential superstar song writer or buying a catalogue of songs, the concentration of a larger proportion of the music publishing industry in a few conglomerates was inevitable. As a result, more songs were bought and sold in the 1980s than in all of the previous years of the business combined.

Presently (1995), Warner/Chappell Music and EMI Music are the two largest publishing companies in the world. Each of these companies is affiliated with a larger conglomerate: Warner/Chappell is owned by the American Time Warner, and EMI Music is owned by the British Thorn–EMI. Their catalogues (each in excess of 500,000 songs) are the result of numerous purchases and/or mergers, largely in the 1980s. Warner Chappell Music resulted from a 1987 merger between Warner Brothers Music and Chappell Music Group, which had itself been sold in 1984 by Polygram Records. EMI Music bought SBK in 1989 for an estimated $337 million for approximately 250,000 songs, which consisted largely of the catalogue of CBS Songs that SBK had acquired in 1986 for an estimated $125 million.

Other major publishing companies today include MCA Music (a division of MCA acquired by Matsushita Electrical Industrial in 1990), Sony Music (formerly CBS music which bought Nashville-based Tree International in 1988 for about $40 million), and BMG Music Publishing (owned by the German multinational corporation, Bertelsmann). There are a number of other significant music publishers that are affiliates of other major companies such as Polygram Music.

Where the structure of the music publishing business differs from that of the recording industry is in the existence of a wide range of independent music publishers. This situation may be largely the result of the difference between the phonogram and music publishing businesses. Labels rely on a distribution system dominated by six companies to sell their products, while a publisher with a hit song can do business with a telephone. Because publishers are not reliant on a distribution system for their business, many more of them are able to survive as independents. The industry also includes a number of private publishing companies owned by song writers such as Bob Dylan, Paul McCartney and Michael Jackson. While it is true that there are a large number of independent publishers, an increasing number of them rely upon the major worldwide publishers to administer their catalogues or to collect income in specific territories.

According to the industry, worldwide music publishing revenues for 1990 were in excess of $3 billion. These revenues were derived from the following sources: small performance rights, mechanical royalties, royalties from printed editions of songs and synchronization rights. The leading source of publishing income in 1990 was performance royalties, which accounted for $1.587 billion. Worldwide mechanical royalties were estimated at $847 million. Print music revenues were $415 million, and the remaining royalties – largely from synchronization – totalled $145 million. The United States accounted for about 35 per cent of the total worldwide, with about $1.056 billion in income. The US breakdown was

$539 million in performance royalties, $300 million in mechanicals, $167 million in print and $50 million in other income. Following the United States in publishing income were Germany ($400 million), France ($370 million), Italy ($240 million), Japan ($240 million), the United Kingdom ($195 million) and Canada ($115 million).

Frith (1987) points out that the monopoly privileges of musical copyright holders are now essential for entertainment corporations' profits. Music as a commodity form (records, CDs, cassettes) doesn't need to be sold to the public at all. Income is generated from the collection of performing rights for music used in films, videos, radio and television programmes and advertisements. As satellite and cable TV continue to rely on music as a cheap source of programme material the question of copyright is destined to become the issue to dominate the entire entertainment industry.

PIRACY

Perhaps the most controversial legal dimension concerning the international music industry is that of piracy. The International Federation of Phonogram and Videogram Producers (IFPI) estimates (see Table 6.1) that 25 per cent of the music phonograms sold throughout the world are pirate copies. In some countries in Asia, Africa, the Middle East and Latin America the proportion of pirate copies is estimated at over 75 per cent (Laing, 1986).

The cheap availability of duplicating machines makes the pirating of already popular music a simple thing. On the international level it is the

Table 6.1 World piracy statistics, 1990: CDs, LPs and cassettes

Region	Units (millions)	Value (millions, US$)
1 Europe (EEC)	21,638,000	147,792,000
2 Europe (non-EEC)	2,381,000	7,582,000
3 Australasia	1,500,000	7,132,000
4 South East Asia	287,061,000	322,051,000
5 Middle East and Mediterranean	23,200,000	58,280,000
6 Africa	23,416,000	45,081,000
7 Latin America	71,677,000	96,223,000
8 North America	46,452,000	423,390,000
Total	477,325,000	1,107,531,000

Source: IFPI,1990

Anglo-American rock stars who are pirated most. Laing claims that, 'piracy's most important effect is not the damage it does to the income of transnational companies and their recording artists, but the way in which it encourages the spread of international music and discourages the full development of national recordings in many countries' (Laing, 1986: 336).

A trade war of enormous magnitude seems set to break out between the USA and China over the pirate copies of American products produced illegally in China. Books, CDs, CD-ROMs, videofilms and computer software are just some of the products being produced on a massive scale in China. The international community seems poised on condemning China's flagrant violation of international patent, copyright and royalty legislation. Modern digital technology means that the pirate copies are as good as the original. Piracy is so widespread that in Peking one can buy the latest music or film release often before they appear on the shelves in America or Europe. The interesting twist is that suddenly China is the world's largest market for music and films!

With the growing popularity of acoustically superior compact discs and the increased diffusion of digital audio tape (DAT), digital compact cassettes (DCCs) and mini discs (MDs) the industry has experienced the virtual 'death of black vinyl'. State of the art pirate manufacturing could conceivably force a change in structure of the entire phonogram industry.

The greatest form of price competition is one the industry has very little control over. 'Home taping is killing music' has been the official industry battle cry since the 1980s. The industry sees home taping as almost as harmful as piracy. This argument is outlined in the official industry report, 'The Case for a Home Taping Royalty' (IFPI, 1984). The report states:

> The inevitable consequence of denying music publishers and record producers any income from unauthorised private copying is to diminish the level of available funds for investment in the promising young artists and writers who could become the megastars of the future. A vicious downward spiral operates here. If less money is available to invest in new talent, there will be a declining number of people who achieve star status. This in turn means that fewer records will be made and sold. The continual shrinkage of money available to invest in new talent must be against the public interest. There are undoubtedly potential Elton Johns – and – Yehudi Menuhins – around the world; but they have no chance of developing and fulfilling their promise if an already difficult and highly competitive working environment is exacerbated by unauthorised private copying.

The IFPI has lobbied aggressively in the major music markets for a levy on blank tapes as a partial solution. The industry position is clear: every blank tape sold means one less CD or cassette sold. This industry position must be considered somewhat misguided. While undoubtedly home taping is having an adverse effect on the sales of prerecorded music, it remains uncertain how damaging a practice it really is. A blank cassette sells for a fraction of what a CD costs. Each blank cassette sold cannot simply be equated with another CD not sold. This denies the logical premise that the cultural sector is an integrated economic whole within which industries and companies compete for a limited pool of disposable income.

Even the industry's own research lends little in the way of support for the 'taping is theft' thesis. In the still most sophisticated survey of home taping undertaken, Kapp *et al.* (1982) point out that those who only tape selections from albums outnumber those who only tape complete albums by two to one and that those who do both kinds of taping account for just over 50 per cent of the time spent taping prerecorded music. Similarly, they demonstrate that tapers were both 'more likely to perceive pre-recorded music as "very important" to them than non-tapers (32% vs. 18%)' and that, in terms of knowledge, attendances at concerts and reading habits, tapers are far more committed to music than non-tapers. In general, these findings suggest that tapers are literally 'active' rather than 'passive' purchasers of music and that, though they are deserting the industry as consumers of prerecorded music, they are not deserting music as such. Also important to note is that active music consumers generally purchase more prerecorded music than the passive consumer (Burnett, 1988b).

Home taping represents a significant change in the patterns of consumption of music, and it can't be stopped either technologically, or by the imposition of a levy (as is the case in Sweden), if only because blank tapes will always be less expensive than the equivalent prerecorded item. While the industry may never have wanted to stop home taping entirely, it certainly has wanted to make money by 'licensing' it. What is really at issue here is the ability of the record industry to control the consumption of music. Something that it has done with varied success over the years.

TECHNOLOGY

Harold Innis (1950, 1951) taught us that the characteristics of any age – knowledge, cultural traits, economic and political organization – are circumscribed and defined by the characteristics of the communication technologies employed in that age. Each technology has a tendency to exert control over space (a space bias) or over time (a time bias). The interplay of the dominant forms of media in any age, with their particular biases, will form the underpinnings for unique forms of social and cultural organization. Marshall McLuhan, for example, writes, 'Societies have always been shaped more by the nature of the media by which men communicate than by the content of the communication' (McLuhan and Fiore, 1967: 15). What both Innis and McLuhan hint at but leave to us to develop is the influence of technology on shaping the content of popular culture.

The advent of communication technology has radically reshaped world popular culture in the latter half of this century. As video, cable and satellite technologies spread their way around the globe it is now easier than ever to disseminate popular culture. The high cost of film, television, phonogram and rock video production together with the low cost of transmission has led to the dissemination of popular cultural products around the world. These products are often 'dumped' on peripheral countries/markets (providing programming at a fraction of the cost of locally made products) after already turning a profit in the core countries/markets. No national organization (be it public or private) can match the massive investment in a series like *Dallas*, a film such as *Star Wars*, or a CD and rock video such as Michael Jackson's *Thriller*.

The break even point on recordings is high, reflecting the high risk nature of the industry. According to figures released by the RIAA, in the 1980s less than one record out of five released sold enough copies to recoup its recording costs. For a major phonogram company, the break even point for sales for a CD is approximately 250,000 copies. As in other segments of the entertainment industry, the record company relies on one or two hit albums to pay for the majority of unsuccessful albums.

Records, cassettes and compact discs are all relatively inexpensive to manufacture. The current retail price difference between cassettes and CDs is an artificial difference. An LP or cassette, when reproduced in quantity, can be made for less than $1 per copy, with the wholesale price between $4 and $5 and the retail price between $9 and $11 (1991 figures). A compact disc can be manufactured for less than a dollar, wholesaled at $11, and sold to the consumer for a list price of between $14 and $15. It is the aesthetic production costs therefore, rather than the manufacturing costs, that account for the greater costs and risks. In addition, the habit of producing videos in connection with new releases has greatly increased overall costs.

As technology has evolved and the sophistication of recording techniques has extended to multitrack digital recording, today's costs of making a technically satisfactory recording can be significant. It is not uncommon for a recording artist to spend between $50,000 and $200,000 recording an album. When promotional, advertising and manufacturing costs are added to these expenses, a record label can easily have invested $500,000 in a recording before selling any copies. The flip side of the new digital technology is that with a sampling synthesizer interfaced with a computer, virtually anyone can create and record high quality musical performances.

Once recorded, the recording can today be released in at least five different formats: conventional LP record, cassette, compact disc, digital compact cassette, or mini disc. The fate of these different formats is unpredictable, but all will probably not survive, with the vinyl record destined to disappear. In addition, the new technologies go beyond these known formats, as it is now possible to transmit copies of digital recordings via digital audio cable services, and the anticipated future medium called the 'celestial or global jukebox', which would beam digital copies of the latest music releases into homes via satellite.

One of the most challenging and difficult aspects of the recording industry is the promotion of records. Traditionally, records were promoted through radio airplay. Charges of 'payola' (pay for play) have been levelled periodically against record labels and radio stations, initially in American congressional investigations in 1959 and 1960 (which led to the downfall of Allan Freed) and most recently in a congressional investigation and grand jury investigation into the hiring of independent record promoters and their involvement with radio stations and radio airplay, as well documented by Dannen (1990). According to Dannen, from the late 1970s throughout much of the 1980s, the record companies spent as much as $50 to $80 million each year on independent promotion. After media pressure in the late 1980s and threat of conviction most major record companies discontinued their use of independent promotion companies. By 1993, however, the labels' self-imposed ban on independent promotion seemed to be diminishing, and most record labels were openly acknowledging their use of independent promotion firms to promote their records but denying that such independent promotion is tied in any way to payola or organized crime.

SAMPLING

Technology further tested the legal and business segments of the music industry in the 1980s when an increasing number of producers began to use digital 'samples' of pre-existing recordings in new records. The samples ranged from a single Phil Collins or John Bonham drum beat or a James Brown scream, to an entire chorus of a song. Record companies, music publishers and artist representatives were faced with traditional licensing methods and copyright law principles of 'copying' and 'fair use' that did not specifically address the issues raised by sampling. While it is the 'song' that is copyrighted it is often the 'sound' that is unique.

Sampling took off in the 1980s when the first electronic samplers were introduced. Unlike synthesizers, which generate tones artificially, samplers record real sounds. Anything audible is eligible: prerecorded music, drumbeats, human voices. Samplers transform these sounds into digital codes, which in turn can be manipulated to produce melodies, rhythm tracks and other sound patterns. Sampling is raising serious legal and ethical issues. 'We're talking here about the ultimate instrument', says a noted musician. 'I think that sampling's effect on music cannot be calculated.' James Brown, the Godfather of Soul, claims, for the record, that he has counted at least 134 examples of artists sampling his music.

With millions of dollars in royalties at stake, sampling has become a legal quagmire. Copyright laws protect a composer from having his or her work duplicated by another musician. But what happens if the second party samples only a few seconds of a melody? Or a few seconds of a drum beat?

An entertainment lawyer noted: 'Sampling is just another instance of the law not keeping up with technology.' Artists and music publishers are struggling to settle disputes out of court by devising elaborate formulas to divide royalties between samplers and samplees. M.C. Hammer avoided any problems by sharing credit with Rick James, who wrote 'Super Freak', before sampling the song for his platinum single, 'U Can't Touch This'. 'Everybody is going to go ahead doing it,' predicts the lawyer, 'except now they're going to get their approvals before they make a record. If you go to somebody after you've got a hit and try to cut a deal, they're going to take you to the cleaners.' The copyright and legal ramifications of sampling remain unresolved and will clearly continue to be a hot area of controversy and confusion.

The future of consumer technology for recording and playing music has been a central concern of the music industry for decades. Issues concerning copyright, industry politics and economics of the marketplace have guided the debate more than quality of sound and consumer interests. CD, DAT, DCC and mini disc each, as technology, represents an advance in consumer electronics. Not all have or will succeed in the general consumer marketplace. This with the exception of the CD of course which has become the consumer industry standard. Consumers clearly cannot afford to invest in several expensive formats at the same time and in fact why should anyone start to collect music on all the different formats? Most music shops don't want to stock recordings in every format as it takes up valuable and expensive retail space.

On the level of successful consumer technology, the 'walkman' first introduced by Sony has changed both listening and buying patterns. Consumers apparently find attractive the increased time shifting listening possibilities afforded by walkman technology. The quality of reproduction and frequency response on a cassette also now more closely approximates that of an album.

Technologically it is the compact disc (CD) that has captured the imagination and interest of the manufacturers of recorded music. The compact disc developed jointly by Philips (Polygram) and Sony was first introduced to the market in 1983. CD did not become the 'overnight success story' that Sony and Polygram had hoped, for several reasons. The major problem was that in 1984 there were only two manufacturing plants in the world, one in West Germany and Japan each, serving Europe, North America and Asia. Another serious problem was the high rejection rate in the actual manufacturing of the compact discs. All sources acknowledge at least an initial 50 per cent rejection rate, although things have improved. To this can be added that there was also consumer reluctance due to the initial high cost of both CD players and the actual discs.

It is safe to say that CD is the revolution in prerecorded music that is now happening around the world. CDs sound better than conventional records and tapes with a greater range of frequency response. Like cassettes, CDs are more convenient and transportable than conventional records. CDs are also virtually indestructible. Perhaps most importantly, CDs have, with very few exceptions, consistently received good press (Hardy, 1985). There are now three types of CD players on the market, the standard stationary model, the CD car player model and the portable CD walkman model.

The latest development in technology now facing the industry is the introduction of digital audio tape (DAT), mini discs (MDs), digital compact cassettes (DCCs), compact disc interactive (CD-I), compact disc read only memory (CD-ROM) and in the near future compact disc erasable (CD-E). DAT cassette recorders and mini disc recorders enable one to make master quality digital recordings. CD-E is a medium that will allow indefinite recording and erasure on compact disc without loss of quality. Both of these new technologies will enable consumers to make perfect 'master' quality copies or reproductions ad infinitum.

The high price of the machines is the only obstacle to be overcome before reaching the mass consumer market. The industry response to these new technologies is reflected by past IFPI President, Ertegun, who commented: 'We have to redouble our efforts to impress on the Japanese hardware manufacturers the huge amount of damage that could be done to our industry, and ultimately to their own, if these systems are marketed without any protection for copyright owners' (IFPI, 1988: 2). The problem is that today the same people own both the hardware and the software.

What about the future of digital recording technology and CDs? There is a surprisingly general consensus amongst music industry officials, audiophiles, as well as artists and home technology freaks. Most believe that custom CDs on demand will be available beginning in 1996. Artist and producer Jerry Harrison predicts that the greatest use for the CD-on-demand technology will be for new artists with unpredictable sales potential and for 'difficult to find albums, which at present would not be profitable to release on CD' (*Wired*, 1994: 12).

When it comes to digital recording studios, most agree that while the transition towards disc-based digital systems is gaining momentum, 'tape has deep roots in this market'. Around the year 2002, digital recording studios will outnumber traditional analog studios. Most experts agree that affordable home CD recorders will be on the home audio market by as early as 1997. While there is little doubt that alternative music distribution will be revolutionized by digital technology, a crucial aspect will be getting consumers 'wired' with the high bandwidth necessary to download music at an acceptable rate. Most experts agree that CDs and CD-ROMs will be around until about the year 2010 when the electronics and music companies push the next generation technology with greater revenue potential. Clearly, the introduction of new technology will continue to be an important battleground for the various actors well into the next century.

MUSIC TELEVISION

Another important development in the record business has been the growth of the music video, particularly as a promotion tool for the sale of albums through outlets like MTV. In addition, extended length videos, concert videos and video compilations have established new sources of revenue and deals for the recording industry through video cassettes, video discs and pay, cable and satellite television licensing.

As radio airplay for new artists has become increasingly difficult to obtain, phonogram companies and artists have sought alternative means of promoting and ultimately selling recordings. Live performance tours have been a traditional promotional vehicle. The advent of MTV and music videos brought an entirely new avenue of record promotions to the industry. As MTV broke new talent and promoted new songs, virtually all major recording artists and labels began to produce music videotapes, primarily for promotion purposes, with the ultimate goal of an audiovisual combination as a new medium in a videocassette or laser disc. The potential of long form music videos has been demonstrated many times over, with it no longer unusual for them selling over and beyond a million copies.

With the introduction of the modern cable and satellite technologies, music videos have increasingly become the new way to listen to music. MTV, which is controlled by media giant Viacom, now claims to reach 320 million households in 90 countries on 5 continents, 24 hours a day. MTV utilizes what we can call the 'universal lingual approach' (Luyken, 1986). That is to say, their music programmes rely very little on the spoken word but use the common language of music and popular culture, supported by a minimum of moderation and small talk by host VJs. The growth of MTV worldwide is impressive: USA 1981, Europe 1987, Brazil 1990, Asia 1991, Japan 1992 and Latin America 1993.

MTV Europe is the fastest growing cable and satellite channel in Europe. The channel's penetration level is limited by Europe's differing cable system: some countries have a firm cable infrastructure; others are somewhat less cabled or hardly connected at all. MTV research shows that Europe's teens consider English the international language of rock 'n' roll.

In music television, the recording business found a marketing tool that brought it unprecedented profits. At the same time, pop music – which had traditionally been too raw and unpolished for television – became one more kind of programming, transformed by the changing needs and visual form of television. As news, sports, movies and politics had capitulated to television, so did nearly every kind of pop music that had ambitions towards mass popularity.

As music critic Jon Pareles explains:

> Because the channel is the equivalent of a national radio network, with the added allure of pictures, MTV's choice of hits has taken on enormous power. With rare exceptions, the price of video production has raised the ante on promoting a pop hit; a video for one song can cost more to make than an entire album ... And in a visual culture like ours, MTV has amplified the importance of image over sound, which has repercussions in everything from stage shows to who gets a chance to record.
>
> (Pareles, 1991: 1)

A concern amongst some artists is that music television has changed the balance of power in favour of the visual image over the music. Pareles notes that:

> MTV favors pretty people ... Ageing performers, or those whose only talents are musical rather than visual, tend to hide in their own video clips, if they get a chance to make them at all. In recent years, record-ing companies have seemed to weigh performers' appearance, fashion sense and dance moves more than in pre-MTV days. The music can be patched together in the studio, while looks are harder to fix. Of course, a cute person can always be hired to lip-synch; ask Milli Vanilli.
>
> (Pareles, 1991: 1)

Music video has also changed the nature of the live concert situation. Before music video, artists and fans faced each other primarily in concerts, with the chance of missed notes or mishaps. Now, the image of a perfor-mance can be fabricated with studio perfect sound and every accessory in place. Many musicians have been willing to sacrifice spontaneity for such security, and in the belief that audiences want to confirm what they've seen on MTV. Many live concert tours have become visual spectacles, where the music might be prerecorded so that the singers can concentrate on dance steps.

Music video also helps build careers so fast that singers like Janet Jackson, Whitney Houston or Mariah Carey end up facing arena or stadium audiences without the experience that would have come from working their way up the circuit. A prominent American record execu-tive says: 'I probably wouldn't be running a record company if MTV didn't exist. This is a business of manipulation. Anyone who denies it is playing a game with you. How do you get a record added to radio? How do you create friends? How do you have relationships? This is a business with a lot of powerful individuals in it' (Goodman, 1991: 41).

It's not enough to simply get a video on MTV: If you're going to sell phonograms, the game is getting quality airtime. 'A video has to be in a good daytime rotation', says another executive. 'You need daytime plays to get attention – at least one good play a day.' The competition is tough: MTV considers between 40 and 60 new videos in an average week and might add three or four to its regular rotation. Thus making the weekly acquisitions and play list meeting at MTV one of the key gatekeeping functions in the industry. An MTV executive said: 'People feel that the best way to compete is to spend a lot of money ... It's easy to spend $200,000 on a video. We don't want people to do that. The biggest videos since I've been here have been low-budget videos ... It's easy to go out and spend money and lay the guilt on MTV.'

The major labels that can afford to make a video and spend the $100,000 needed to effectively promote a single are even less inclined to take chances than MTV is. And everything MTV takes a chance on that becomes a hit is instantly mimicked by every other label, creating a 'copy cat' mentality. 'We get 20 versions of the same thing every week, ' claimed the same MTV executive. 'As soon as Seal comes out and we love it, there are 12 Seals. As soon as Poison comes out and they're big, you have 19 hair bands that look like Poison.'

Depending how you view things, MTV is the simultaneous fulfilment of every threat and promise in media theory since Walter Benjamin first came to reflect upon the work of art in the age of mechanical reproduction.

THE CONSTRAINTS IN CONCERT

The influences that changes in law, technology, market, industry and organizational structure have on the modern phonogram industry have been documented. As noted, these constraints seldom operate alone or in isolation. In fact, they usually work in concert in some form of interaction. Together the constraints help to illuminate the complexity of the contemporary phonogram industry. It is an industry that in the 1990s consists of a corporate centre or core (Big Six), involved in the production of multimedia entertainment on a worldwide basis, and a periphery of local and national music and media scenes. The changing nature of the relationship between the core and the periphery and between generalist firms and specialist firms, from one of competition to one of cooperation, is one of the major topics of the following chapters.

Chapter 7

The American example

Businessmen, they drink my wine.
(Bob Dylan, 'All Along the Watchtower')

The importance of the American popular music industry should not be underestimated. As noted earlier, it is by far the largest single market in terms of sales in the world. The fact remains that the output of the popular music industry in North America constitutes the majority input of those radio and television formats around the world that rely on popular music for programme content. The levels of industry concentration and musical innovation and diversity affect not only the range of choice offered to the consumer in the retail stores but also determines to a large extent what audiences hear on the radio and see on the television. With deregulation sweeping across Europe this is not unimportant. Also important is the fact that due to the extreme commercial nature of the American music industry there exists a whole sub-industry that conducts media performance and audience research. Hence there exists an overwhelming abundance of data available for secondary analysis.

What has happened to musical diversity during the latest period of further industry concentration? Are more or less songs making it into the popularity charts? Are new artists being shut out of the charts? Is there a relationship between the level of industry concentration and the level of musical diversity? These are some of the questions I will address in this chapter. First I take up the question of concentration and diversity as well as cycles of music production. Then using empirical material from the Billboard charts, a historical analysis of the American popular music industry is developed that partially addresses these and other important questions.

CYCLES IN MUSICAL PRODUCTION

The immense literature on cultural, political, economic and social cycles indicate a widespread interest and concern with cycles in the social sciences. Furthermore, cycles have proved to be elusive phenomena, the search for which can be likened to the search for the golden fleece. As Weber (1987) has pointed out, the term 'cycle' has been used both as a meaningless term of convenience associated with almost any sort of fluctuation over time, and as a term referring to several specific aspects of changes over time that meet specific tests. Weber goes on to distinguish between weak, moderate and strong forms of the cycle concept which he refers to as the first, second and third kind of cycle concept, respectively, based upon whether the cycle concept is applied to empirical phenomena or to theoretical arguments and the extent to which the cycle concept is decomposed into its constituent elements (Weber, 1987: 146).

In the literature on popular music several examples can be found that stretch the use of the cycle concept. On the basis of the interplay between musical communities and the marketplace Ash (1980) describes four eras or 'waves'. The first wave (1955–1958) is when the music of the urban communities reached a mass audience. The second period (1959–1963) was the counter-reformation and the search for the magic formula by the industry. The next period (1963–1969) was the 'second wave' and the return of the music of the urban communities. The final period for Ash is simply the 'seventies' when music apparently stagnated. Ash's study is both enlightening and frustrating. A good deal of insight is shown in his description of the interplay between the urban musical communities and the marketplace. Sorely missed is any attempt to incorporate any of the wealth of available economic material that could bolster the arguments.

In another study of the American popular music industry, Shore (1983) discusses five eras whose boundaries have more to do with presentation considerations than with theory or cycles. These five eras are: first, 1877 to 1921; second, 1922 to 1950; third, the 1950s to 1963; fourth, 1964 to the early 1970s; and finally, the 1970s. For each era Shore attempts to describe the interaction between the industry, the technology and the music. A major weakness of Shore's study is the lack of incorporation of previous research which addresses the same time period.

In a qualitative and quantitative analysis of the 15 most popular recorded singles each year between 1955 and 1982, Chesebro et al. (1985) discern five patterns or eras of popular music. The first era (1955–1959) is the 'Era of Interpersonal Romance', characterized by the concern for interpersonal issues cast in romanticized terms. The second era

(1959–1964) is the 'Era of Dynamic Equilibrium', noted for its greater range, balance and variety of musical symbols. The third era (1965–1973), the 'Era of Ironic Leadership', is dominated by themes of irony and leader-centred concepts. The fourth era (1974–1979) is the 'Era of Ironic Romance', characterized by the dominance of irony and romantic themes. The fifth era (1980–1982) is the 'Era of Pragmatic Skepticism' noted for the balanced tension between themes of cynicism, leadership and romance. While at times fascinating, the major weakness of the study is the lack of any attempt to link the observed changes in lyrical content to changes in the music industry in general.

In an interesting study of the characteristics of the Billboard charts, Feihl (1981) delineates five cycles of rock music. The five cycles are: the birth of rock 'n' roll (1954–1957), the development of rock 'n' roll (1958–1963), the British invasion (1964–1965), the development of rock (1966–1974) and the disco trend (1975–1977).

By examining the Top 100 charts Feihl shows that each of the five cycles to some extent are marked by an increase, a peak and finally a decrease in the total number of charted entries. A major strength of Feihl's study is the incorporation of qualitative information on musical styles and trends that helps to explain the statistical changes from cycle to cycle. This combination of data makes for a thorough study with many useful starting points for future research.

THE AMERICAN EXAMPLE

Economists have long been concerned with the question of the relationship between product innovation and market structure. Since Schumpeter (1950) most have argued that innovation will more often occur in an oligopolistic market structure. It was thought that under oligopolistic conditions firms were better able to afford and finance innovation and pass the cost benefits along to the consumer. More recent evidence shows that this is not the case, and instead suggests a negative relationship between product diversity and oligopolistic market control (Scherer, 1970/1980; Steele, 1975; Rogers and Rogers, 1976).

In a review of the literature concerning the production of culture in America, Ryan (1985) observes that:

> This body of research suggests that as long as an organization finds itself in a relatively stable environment; that is, a lack of competitors and stable relations at input and output boundaries, the organization is likely to attempt to maintain the status quo. This is often done by

developing products aimed at not offending any group of consumers. Almost invariably, this tactic leads to a high level of product homogeneity which does in fact alienate portions of the consuming market. If the alienated segment becomes large enough, newer firms or firms out of the mainstream are able, through product innovation, to make inroads into the market.

(Ryan, 1985: 4)

The majority of the research on concentration and diversity focuses on non-symbol-producing firms. The few studies focusing on culture-producing firms have obtained similar results. For example, Peterson and Berger (1975) show that in the period 1948–1973, there is a negative (perhaps cyclical) relationship between concentration and diversity in the recording industry; specifically, as the proportion of top selling records sold by the leading firms increases, the number of best selling records decreases. Conversely, as the number of different best selling records increases, fewer of these records are sold by the leading firms. Rothenbuhler and Dimmick (1982) show that this relationship continued to hold between 1974 and 1980.

DiMaggio (1977) extends this model to book publishing and the film industry, while arguing that it is an empirical generalization that can be applied to the production and consumption of diverse cultural products. In addition, studies of television (Dominick and Pierce, 1976), film (Guback, 1969; Jowett and Linton, 1980) and book publishing (Coser *et al.*, 1982) show that in these industries concentration and diversity are inversely related. That is to say, that periods of market concentration alternate with periods of competition, with the former being associated with product homogeneity and the latter with diversity. This orthodox view can roughly be presented as shown in Figure 7.1.

Nord (1980) finds this relationship between market concentration and product diversity to hold across other industries:

The greater the market power a producer has (the greater the opportunity to control risk) the tighter and more standardized will be the formulas ... The business history of book and magazine publishing, film making, song selling, comic stripping and radio and television broadcasting provides evidence in support of this hypothesis.

(Nord, 1980: 215)

It is interesting to examine the relationship between concentration and diversity in terms of our 'resource partitioning model' in which producers and consumers are divided between generalist and specialist firms. As

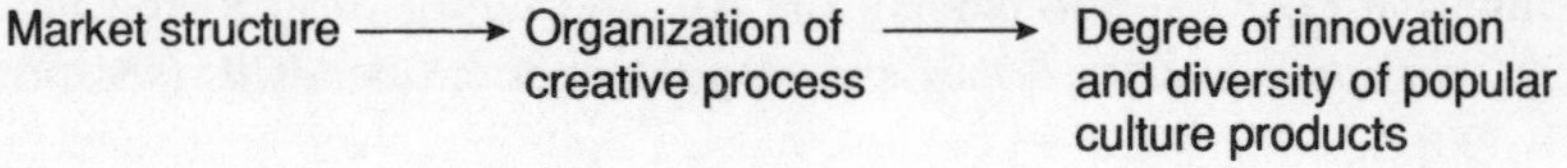

Market structure ———→ Organization of ———→ Degree of innovation
                        creative process   and diversity of popular
                                                 culture products

Figure 7.1 Orthodox view

Source: DiMaggio, 1977; Lewis, 1978

noted earlier, as concentration increases and as the large, generalist firms produce more homogeneous products, they create opportunities for more innovative and specialized firms whose products appeal to more narrow markets. However, as their products gain marketshares, these specialized firms are absorbed by larger firms, thereby increasing concentration and again creating new opportunities for smaller firms.

Why then is the concentration level of the American music industry of interest? As noted above, numerous observers of the American popular music industry have repeatedly discussed the relationship between industry concentration and musical diversity. These investigators often employ cyclical models to describe changes in the music industry. One basic idea is that there are steady waves of change within the production system. This cyclical model also holds that there is constant and inherent conflict between bigger and smaller producers. Various studies have shown that smaller record labels and independent entrepreneurs respond more quickly and are more encouraging of musical change than are larger companies. The major record labels have always been a step behind while looking for the 'lowest common denominator', more interested in confirming tastes than disrupting them. Musical creativity and industry innovation, on this view, results from the entrepreneurs 'getting lucky' with their risk capital paying off. The major labels then move in after the fact and the independents are bought out or driven out through competitive pricing resulting from economies of scale or through more lucrative contracts to the artists. This is part of what we can call the 'old popular music model'.

This model also holds that the market structure of an industry, particularly the level of market concentration, determines the degree of control over the market that firms hold. This control of the market then strongly influences the independence granted to popular culture creators which in turn affects the degree of innovation and diversity in the products that are produced. The resulting picture views the major

companies steering innovation and diversity from above. These arguments have been used to explain the rise and fall of rock 'n' roll in the
1950s, rock music in the 1960s and of punk rock in the 1970s (see Frith,
1981: 90).

There are several assumptions implicit in this model (see DiMaggio,
1977; Lewis, 1978). First, as pointed out above, this model rightly assumes
that managers of organizations place great value on predictability. This
occurs whether the product is records, books, newspapers or automobiles.
The establishment of stable routines, procedures, communication channels
and working relationships ensure continued performance and minimize
risk and conflict. Second, as often documented for the music industry, the
old model assumes that demand for diversity will usually exceed the
supply. Third, it assumes that most creators of culture in contemporary
society have a creative desire to innovate, to generate new cultural forms
and content. A number of studies have documented the conflict between
creators and managers over the issue of creativity and control (e.g. Becker,
1982; Coser *et al.*, 1982).

If these basic assumptions are correct then the dilemmas facing
managers in the popular culture industry are twofold. First, they must
control their markets by maintaining enough economic power to prevent
competitors from entering the market and satisfying latent demand
(Hirsch, 1972; DiMaggio, 1977). Second, they must control their own
creative divisions so that creation remains routine, predictable and guar-
anteed to produce a product acceptable to the widest range of consumers
in the controlled marketplace. That is to say, to produce the product that
will please the most and offend the least number of consumers (see
DeFleur and Ball-Rokeach, 1988).

However, the traditional model doesn't account for the diverse and ever
changing nature of public taste; it fails to address questions concerning
new trends, new demands by the public or satisfaction of the audience.
The new model discussed below in part addresses these issues because it
investigates reciprocal causation rather than the one-way causality asserted
in the old model. This mutual causality or reciprocal relationship suggests
that the major companies indeed don't control the market from above
and perhaps are just as much controlled from below. Implicit in this
idea is the suggestion that the major companies and the independents no
longer compete but cooperate instead, based on a relationship of 'symbiotic mutualism'.

According to the traditional model, the majors would take over the
entire production system in order to control the music itself. However,
the majors no longer exclusively pursue this kind of policy (Burnett, 1988a).

The majors have passed from production contracts to distribution contracts which are more profitable to both sides. As Hellman (1983) explains:

> the pattern is rather that the smaller companies offer a test market for the competition between the larger companies, through which these companies can outline their musical production. The smaller companies have gained a permanent and important though subordinate position in the music industry. The cycles have changed into symbiosis. The new state of competition has to some extent created a music culture richer in variations.
>
> (Hellman, 1983: 355)

In 1992 the dominance of the transnationals in the manufacturing and/or distributing of phonograms in the USA became clear. The largest share of the market in 1992 was accounted for by Warner and its various labels with 27 per cent of all phonograms. The second largest manufacturer/ distributor was Sony with 25 per cent of the entire market. Next came EMI with 15 per cent, MCA with 12 per cent, BMG with 9 per cent and Polygram with 5 per cent (IFPI, 1993). Remaining independent companies accounted for just 7 per cent of total phonogram market shares.

THE HISTORICAL ACCOUNT

In the Peterson and Berger (1975) account, the time since 1948 is divided into several periods, each characterized by qualitatively different relations between concentration and diversity. Their approach consists of providing a description of the historical changes in the popular music industry, American culture generally, and in the mass media, both content and institutions. Here one can briefly summarize and extend their interpretations and explanations.

The period 1948–1955 is one of high *corporate concentration* (ibid.: 160–161). In this interval, concentration is high but slowly declining. Major producers attempted to maintain high control over the market through vertical integration, that is, through the control of the total production flow from raw materials to wholesale sales. The top firms also tried to reduce competition by attempting to monopolize artistic factors, controlling the media of merchandising, and the channels of distribution, and through cover records. (A cover record was when a major company had their own artists record a hit song of a competitor, thus cashing in on the tune's established popularity.) This was also a period of relative homogeneity of cultural (pop musical) products (ibid.: 162–164). Peterson and Berger note that two studies found that, 'over 80 per cent of all songs fit into a conventionalized love cycle where sexual references are allegorical and social problems are unknown'. At the time the system was efficient and economical for the companies and provided acceptable sales growth. The industry reflected characteristics of other American industries at the time: production concentrated in a few firms, vertical integration, routine production and little innovativeness.

The mid to late 1950s (1956–1959) is a period of stronger *competition*, as indicated by lower concentration ratios and higher diversity (ibid.: 164–166). The major producers lost their commanding position because of the introduction by several independent companies of guitar-based rock 'n' roll music. The success of the independent labels was caused in turn by a change in radio station format from dramatic programmes to recorded music. Citing Hirsch (1970), Peterson and Berger argue that this change in radio format resulted from the shift during this period of advertising revenue from radio to television. Consequently, radio stations developed a new format in which less expensive recorded popular music replaced more expensive network and syndicated radio programmes. This is also the period when the LP and cheap transistor radios became popular. Increased competition between radio stations meant that the audience was gradually no longer defined as a mass audience but as a number of discrete groups with differing tastes. The latent tastes of the audience were soon picked up on by the stations who in turn selected a particular type of music and played it exclusively. This was a 'boom time' period for the industry when diversity increased, the number of cover records dropped to zero, the number of new artists doubled and record sales soared. The industry concentration ratio dropped drastically with independent labels reaping most of the increase in profits. The majors also benefited from the release of suppressed musical tastes as their profits also increased, although not substantially.

The next, *secondary consolidation*, phase in the historical development of the popular music industry spanned 1960–1963 and was characterized by the expansion of the market in terms of total sales, combined with the rise of new leading firms. The four-firm concentration ratio declined to 25 per cent while the eight-firm ratio held at about 50 per cent. The market share of individual firms changed rapidly from year to year (ibid.: 166). Some independents grew large and the total number of firms stabilized. The market was slow and the majors decided that the new rock 'n' roll sounds were not a fad and bought up the contracts of established artists and sometimes successfully picked and promoted new ones.

As a result of the 'British invasion' and 'Beatlemania', the next six-year period (1964–1969) was one of *renewed growth*. Diversity peaked and concentration increased substantially. Sales volumes also increased (ibid.: 167). Peterson and Berger also suggest that diversity should have peaked during the 1960–1963 period when concentration was at its lowest point (since 1948). They interpret the results for the renewed growth period as indicating a three year lag of diversity behind concentration. This is an important observation which we will have cause to return to below.

Concentration returned to relatively high levels and diversity declined to relatively low levels in the *reconstruction* period, 1970–1973. Major firms displaced independents as industry leaders, either through buying the contracts of important acts, or by acquiring one or more independent record companies (ibid.: 168). Diversity fell in this period also. How did the majors regain control of the market? First, they increased central control over the creative process through deliberate creation and extensive promotion of new artists, long-term contracts and reduced autonomy for producers. The majors also consolidated their leading position in the manufacturing and distribution of recordings. During the period the majors also made extensive use of illegal promotion such as payola (the playing of records on the radio for cash) and legal promotion which the independents could not match.

Following Peterson and Berger's methods, Rothenbuhler and Dimmick (1982) analysed the relationship between concentration and diversity between 1974 and 1980. In this *regained concentration* period, the number of firms competing in the popular music market declined. They also found that concentration rose to its highest levels since the 1948–1955 period and diversity declined substantially. During this period the majors were able to exert further control over the creative process and marketing. Rothenbuhler and Dimmick conclude that, 'as the number of competing firms declines, so does the number of hit records' (ibid.: 143), consequently, consumers found fewer choices in the marketplace. (For a detailed statistical account of the period 1948–1989, see Burnett, 1990a, 1992b.)

A DECADE OF TRANSITION

What then happened during the 1980s? Has the industry remained in control and stabilized and consolidated the 'vagaries of public tastes'? In the *transition* period, 1981–1990, one finds that concentration remained at historically high levels but diversity increased substantially, yielding a configuration unique since 1948 in which both concentration and diversity are high. This would appear to refute earlier claims that the degree of diversity in musical form is inversely related to the degree of market concentration. Also the increase in the number of records making the charts was matched by an increase in the number of new artists reaching the charts. This would imply that new artists are being infused into the system. The evidence reported here thus suggests that despite high concentration there has been more variety (more songs and new artists) in popular music. Hence the audience has been exposed to a wider range of music, thus refuting the predictions of homogeneity and trivialization posited by Horkheimer and Adorno (1972) and Koval (1988).

What accounts for these new and different findings? It will be argued below that the record industry, at least temporarily, has found the key to a system in which both concentration and diversity remain high. This trend is driven by structural changes in the marketplace and among producers and consumers. Specifically, the record industry is making the transition from a youthful or nascent industry into that of a mature industry. Transition to industry maturity often signals a number of important changes in the competitive environment. Porter (1980: 283) outlines the most common tendencies in industry maturity which we can apply to the phonogram industry as follows.

1 Slowing growth means more competition for market share. In the 1980s when the phonogram companies were unable to maintain historical growth rates merely by holding market share, competitive attention turned inward to attacking the shares of others. This was mostly achieved by the direct takeover of smaller firms and labels as well as the signing of contracts with artists on competing labels.
2 Firms in the industry increasingly are selling to experienced, repeat buyers. The demographic base of phonogram consumers has expanded as people continue to listen to pop and rock music long into middle age. In effect, the industry has managed to sell people music that they already own by putting out entire back catalogues on CD. These re-releases account for almost half of all CD sales.
3 There is a topping out problem in adding industry capacity and personnel. As the phonogram industry has adjusted to slower growth, the adding of capacity and personnel has come to a standstill. The transnationals have rationalized the production process to the extent that they have far fewer employees now than in the 1970s.
4 Manufacturing, marketing, distributing, selling and research methods are often undergoing change. This is a major area of change in the phonogram industry. In fact, one can hazard to say that recent developments are changing the basic structure of the industry. Most notable are the increased distribution channels for music via the increase in radio stations, cable and satellite TV and of course music television.

5 New products and applications are harder to provide. The ability to come up with new products and applications becomes increasingly difficult as costs and risks increase during industry maturity. The technology or hardware side of the industry has continually presented new products, the latest being the walkman, the CD player, the DAT recorder, the video disc, the DCC recorder and the mini disc.

6 International competition increases. Technological maturity and product standardization often mark the emergence of significant international competition. In their ongoing effort to keep music vital, the transnationals have expanded operations worldwide and in cooperation with their national affiliates are delving into the 'international talent pool' (see Frith, 1988b) to infuse new artists into the international music charts. This partially explains the international success of 'world music'.

7 Industry profits often fall during the transition period, sometimes temporarily and sometimes permanently. Porter (1980: 240) explains that: 'slowing growth, more sophisticated buyers, more emphasis on market share, and the uncertainties and difficulties of the required strategic changes usually mean that industry profits fall'. All levels of the industry have been affected by declining profit margins in the late 1980s during a period when sales have increased. This has been the result of a rise in R&D costs, marketing costs and royalty payments. This helps explain why so many firms have been sold or taken over by larger media conglomerates.

Several other factors also point to this transition. First, as indicated by yearly sales figures, the industry's steady expansion stopped in the late 1970s (Table 7.1) and did not pick up again until the mid-1980s. Fluctuations in total sales figures in the 1980s have had more to do with price increases via the introduction of the more expensive CD than with total unit sales. As can be seen in Table 7.1 total unit sales peaked in 1992 as the value sales in dollars also continued to rise. Note also the decline of LP albums. The decline of the LP coincides with the increase in sales of the music cassette and the CD. The introduction of CD singles has revived interest and sales of singles again.

The Big Six transnationals have a variety of artists under contract to their various American subsidiary labels, enabling them to take advantage of every new change in musical style. In the attempt to control the environment,the transnationals produce what Garnham (1987) calls 'repertoires' of products. This is one way of dealing with the fact that they can't predict which of their commodities will be purchased by which segment

Table 7.1 Phonogram sales in the USA

	Units in the USA (millions)					
Year	Singles	LP	MC	CD	Total	Value $ (millions)
1973	228	280	15	—	523	1,436
1974	204	276	15	—	495	2,200
1975	164	257	16	—	437	2,360
1976	190	273	22	—	485	2,737
1977	190	344	37	—	571	3,500
1978	190	341	61	—	592	4,131
1979	196	318	83	—	597	3,685
1980	164	323	110	—	597	3,682
1981	155	296	137	—	588	3,626
1982	137	244	182	—	563	3,592
1983	125	210	237	1	573	3,815
1984	131	205	332	6	674	4,370
1985	121	167	339	23	650	4,389
1986	94	125	345	53	617	4,651
1987	82	107	410	102	701	5,567
1988	90	72	450	150	762	6,255
1989	37	35	446	207	725	6,464
1990	28	12	442	287	769	7,541
1991	97	5	360	333	795	7,716
1992	112	2	366	408	888	8,867

Source: IFPI, 1993

of the audience. This also helps to partially account for the rise in diversity as well. Just as important is the fact that the major labels and the independents certainly no longer compete. As was discussed above, this new business relationship entails cooperation between big and small, with the independents often moulding new acts and then making licensing and distribution deals with the majors. The independents are increasingly specialist labels that often deal with fringe genres of music which, in turn, with proper promotion, can become hits. It is also clear that during the 1980s the development of new technologies of both production and consumption have had a liberating effect on the creative process. With the high quality of inexpensive recording equipment it is now possible for groups virtually 'off the street' to produce at least technically high quality music.

What can we conclude from our historical account? In a concise review of the American recording industry, Perrow (1986) notes that several observations can be made. First, it can be noted that the industry seeks to control its environment, not be controlled by it. Companies do adjust to environmental changes, such as technological developments (CDs) and product substitution (MTV for radio), but the drive is to control and manipulate the environment.

Second, it is clear that 'new technological developments do not determine cultural outcomes' (ibid.: 188). Indeed, 'mass markets and cultural homogeneity are not due to the invention of the radio or records or TV; all three are compatible with diversified, segmented markets that reflect diverse cultural styles and interests'. The way in which new technologies are used by the transnationals can create 'massification' while at the same time releasing creative possibilities for consumers. To at least a partial extent the industry has brought a good deal of 'turbulence' into the system in its efforts to introduce innovations such as CDs, walkmans, mini discs, DAT and laser discs.

Third, it is clear that the most salient environment is one containing other transnationals as, 'despite competition among them, they collectively evolve strategies to eliminate or absorb threatening independents'. Finally, it can be noted that the 'costs of turbulence and change, when they occur, are externalized to dependent parts of the industry and thus are borne by artists, producers, and other creative people, or satellite firms that provide standby facilities' (ibid.: 189). The transnationals seldom show a decline in profits during turbulent times but instead pass the costs on.

How do the changes in the 1980s relate to the musical diversity problematic? As noted earlier, proponents of the homogenization thesis (Rothenbuhler and Dimmick, 1982; Koval, 1988) have claimed a trend towards longevity on the hit charts. They also claim that there are fewer songs with longer stays on the charts. Koval notes that fewer new artists made the charts in the early 1980s than did in the mid-1960s. He also claims that the peak of quantitative musical diversity was during the period 1965–1967, while the years 1980–1982 were the least diverse.

Mondak (1989) suggests that one must also examine the average number of hits per artist before making any claims on the health of musical culture. In Table 7.2 data for the periods 1965–1967 and 1980–1982 as well as 1987–1989 are presented. The first period represents a situation with low concentration and high diversity, the second is a period of high concentration and low diversity, while the third represents the unique situation of high concentration and high diversity coinciding.

As can be seen, the figures offer little support for the homogeneity thesis. In fact, only the average number of Hot 100 singles per year has dropped dramatically from 733 in the first period to 440 in the third. This

Table 7.2 Statistical trends on the Billboard charts

	1965–1967	1980–1982	1987–1989
Average no. of Top 10 singles per year	113	76	114
Average no. of Hot 100 singles per year	733	434	440
Average no. new artists with Hot 100 singles per year	88	38	66
Average no. of artists with Hot 100 singles per year	344	296	321
Average no. of Hot 100 songs per artist per year	2.13	1.47	1.37

Source: 1965–1967, 1980–1982: Mondak, 1989. 1987–1989: Burnett, 1990a

could be the result of the transnationals releasing fewer albums each year. The average number of Top 10 singles per year dropped from 113 in the first period to 76 in the second period only to rise to 114 in the third period. A similar pattern can be seen in the average number of new artists with Hot 100 singles per year. In the first period we have 88 new artists, then a drop to 38 in the second period and then a rise to 66 in the third period. The pattern for the average number of artists with Hot 100 singles is much the same, starting with 344 in the first period, then dropping to 296 in the second, only to rise again to 321 in the third period.

The most profound change is shown in the last row of Table 7.2, the average number of Hot 100 songs per artist per year. Here we see a reduction in the average number of hits per artist from 2.13 in the first period to 1.47 in the second, to 1.37 in the third period. Here we can agree with Mondak's (1989: 47) interpretation that, 'the quantitative diversity of speakers declined little as the decrease in the number of Top 100 songs acted mostly to prevent artist-by-artist repetition of form'. What this means then is that we find little support, at least quantitatively, for the homogenization thesis. In fact, more artistic voices are being heard, albeit for shorter lengths of time.

The foregoing account is largely descriptive rather than explanatory. There should be no quarrel with the historical account given by Peterson and Berger (1975) and by Rothenbuhler and Dimmick (1982). However, there are three main difficulties with this type of account. First, it cannot be used to explain the future since the constraints that affect the production and consumption of culture tend to be unique during each period or epoch, and therefore are unlikely to occur again in exactly the same configuration. Second, it does not explicitly attribute to the producers the ability to adapt to changing conditions, to anticipate the future and to remove or alter the various constraints on the production of culture. Third, it says very little about the power of the audience, the consumers who keep the system dynamic. These are some of the very important questions that are left unturned for future research.

THE 1990s, HIT LISTS AND MUSICAL STYLES

In May 1991 Billboard started publishing a new type of album chart, using information from the New York-based Soundscan company. Soundscan monitored record sales in shops and sold the information to record companies. They do this by registering the information from electronic cash registers that read bar codes on records. The data are now collected from a wide range of stores, amounting to what Soundscan claims represents 55 per cent of the US market.

The new Billboard album chart that resulted from the new data made it abundantly clear that the old method of collecting information was flawed. The new chart revealed that country and western, heavy metal and rap music were much more popular than previously assumed. One country artist, Garth Brooks, seemed to singlehandedly rule the charts for several months. Another interesting result was that albums started suddenly appearing at the top of the charts and then quickly dropping out of sight. The old familiar slow climb to the top of the charts and the gradual sliding down was nowhere to be seen, probably an aberration created by poor information.

The new Billboard singles chart is compiled from Soundscan sales data and information about airplay from Broadcast Data Systems of New York. This combined information of how much a single is selling and how much it is being played by radio stations is valuable for the phonogram companies. By knowing where a record is being bought, what sort of audience is buying it, and where they are listening to it, a phonogram company can aim their advertising and promotion at the right people at the right time, and can gain much insight into the trends in musical tastes.

This is especially important when one considers that the phonogram companies may soon be out of the manufacturing business. In future they will be more concerned with the producing and marketing of music. This requires of course that consumers have a way to order and pay for music. Digital radio and two-way cable television are such possibilities. Another is letting consumers order or make their own copies at distribution centres which may be the future role of record stores. The point is the music companies will have to maintain control of distribution in order to profit from the new technology. This helps account for the eagerness of the transnationals in distributing the music of the independent labels.

It was argued above that one of the most important findings of production of culture research is that increased competition in the form of new firms entering the market generally leads to greater product diversity in cultural industries. If the competition equals diversity hypothesis holds, then the decrease in competition by way of the lack of new firms in the market should have led to decreased diversity in popular music. To test this hypothesis an attempt was made to reconsider and update a classic study in the sociology of culture, which noted an inverse relationship between concentration and diversity in the American popular music industry. It was found that this negative relationship persisted into the early 1980s but has since broken down. The American music industry entered the 1990s in a period of both high market concentration and high diversity.

The empirical evidence thus no longer supports the 'old popular music model', even though the main actors continue to control the market. Today they are continually forced to present new styles and new artists to maintain their dominance. A growing international youth market and an ageing rock audience have fundamentally helped to change the way the phonogram industry works. The cyclical model is unable to explain this new situation. The 'new popular music model' must take into account that thousands of small independent or alternative labels help produce the music, in symbiosis with the transnationals, who in turn must sell to a differentiated audience. Thus the transnationals are able to respond more rapidly to the latest trends in music and youth culture. To further facilitate a shorter response time they have developed semi-independent production units and speciality record labels in an attempt to be more artist and consumer friendly. It is important to remember that the multiple in-house labels and contracted independents all use the same phonogram pressing plants, marketing, promotion and distribution organizations that are owned by the transnationals.

Lopes (1992) points out two major advantages of the 'open' system of production. First, the majors benefit financially from monopolizing the end process of popular music production and distribution. Second, the majors can take advantage of the independent producers' autonomy to 'respond to the "unpredictability" of the music market and ensure that successful new artists and musical styles are quickly incorporated into the popular music market they effectively control' (1992: 57).

Most importantly, the independents can also lift essentially marginal musics into the public sphere, where they are reworked by the transnationals for the larger market. This process helps explain how styles such as rap, techno, heavy metal and grunge can be heard in the most unlikely places.

The combination of active independent companies and knowledgeable active music fans has helped to make the transnationals, and indeed our musical sphere, more multifaceted and diverse. Remember that in the 1990s the number one slot in the Billboard album charts has been held by artists as diverse as Metallica (heavy metal), Michael Jackson (pop), Garth Brooks (country), Nirvana (grunge), Aerosmith (rock), Snoop Doggy Dogg (rap) and Ace of Base (Swedish pop).

WHY THE CHANGE IS INTERESTING

One of the central arguments in this book has been that the transnational major phonogram companies through embracing an 'open' system of development and production have produced significant levels of innovation and diversity in contemporary popular music. This in spite of the fact that just six transnationals have effective and unchallenged oligopolistic control of the phonogram industry worldwide.

The contemporary strategy of the transnationals relies on their exclusive control over large-scale manufacturing, distribution and access to the principal avenues of exposure. With this exclusive control, the transnationals have adopted a multidivisional corporate form linked with a large number of independent producers. This open system of development and production remains under oligopolistic conditions because the transnationals find it advantageous to incorporate new artists, producers and styles of music in order to constantly reinvigorate the popular music market and ensure that no large unsated demand among consumers materializes. The innovation and diversity sustained in this open system is essential in order to maintain a profitable and secure market.

The contemporary popular music industry demonstrates that large culture industries, even under oligopolistic conditions, can provide a significant level of innovation and diversity. It has been demonstrated in this and other studies (Burnett, 1990a, 1992b; Hellman and Soramäki, 1994; Lopes, 1992) that the level of innovation and diversity under conditions of high market concentration depends to a large extent on the system of development and production used by the large cultural industries and how these industries structure their markets. Large culture industries that use a closed system of development and production, geared towards a limited mass market, tend to produce generally homogeneous and standardized cultural products. Large culture industries that use an open system of development and production aimed at a loosely segmented market tend to incorporate innovation and diversity as an effective strategy in maintaining the viability of their market. As Lopes (1992) has also noted, high market concentration produces no single, inevitable effect on innovation and diversity in large culture industries; instead, the effect of high market concentration depends on the organization of the specific industry and the structure of its market.

Thus the present study suggests a somewhat new way of viewing the competition and diversity relationship. Previous studies have argued that diversity of products results from competition among firms for consumers. While this study does not dispute those previous findings, it does suggest that competition among firms for scarce resources can lead to increased product diversity and innovation in a period of high market concentration. The Big Six transnationals are constantly searching for an available but unexploited supply of popular music resources in the face of monopolization. Uncertain market environments are usually conceived of in terms of uncertainty of demand. If consumer demand is not met, consumers may simply withdraw from the marketplace. Consequently, the major concern of the phonogram industry is orderly and manageable consumption. It follows that, underlying most phonogram industry practice, is 'the fear of an active audience, whose tastes can't be predicted, whose use of music can't be completely controlled' (Frith, 1981: 270). As a result, corporate uncertainty and fear of the audience withdrawing from the marketplace help to propel the system of concentration and diversity. This also helps to explain why the transnationals are currently pursuing a policy of offering a wide variety of musical genres and an extensive list of products for consumers.

PIONEERS AND SETTLERS

The recent trend towards deregulation in communication has encouraged growth through merger and acquisition. In fact, each of the six major phonogram companies is itself a subsidiary of an even larger electronics or communications conglomerate. This fact is noted by Porter (1980: 287), who points out that, 'few industries begin as global industries, but they tend to evolve into them over time'. There are several common characteristics exemplifying global industries. Most important are: the increased scale economies, decreased transportation and storage costs, rationalized distribution channels and reduced government constraints. All of these trends are present in today's increasingly global phonogram industry.

The trend towards bigness in the media, especially the concentration of ownership through mergers and acquisitions, creates enormous financial and people resources for media companies. As the communication conglomerates grow, we can expect an intensification of cross-media activities in the struggle for audiences in the ever more fractionalized 'mediascape' of the 1990s. Today's entertainment conglomerates sell both the software and the hardware while their various companies and departments produce 'tie-ins' between books, films, records and videos that in essence advertise and help to sell each other. In an industry characterized by uncertainty, economies of multiformity may lessen risk and thereby promote survival of these organizations. As Dimmick (1986) has also noted, economies of multiformity are the result of the operations of individual firms in more than one communications industry, a trend conspicuously obvious in the record industry.

It was earlier mentioned that one aspect of bigness is the increasing emphasis on producing big sellers: 'blockbuster' or 'mega' hits. Music companies that are purchased by multimedia conglomerates come under increasing pressure to produce large profits. Marketing recordings with enormous sales potential is a quick way to respond to that demand. The emphasis on multimedia tie-ins is another important part of this trend. One result of this increased emphasis on marketing products to create huge sales is a change in the balance of power in music companies. The influence of marketing, promotion and sales departments increases, and the importance of creative people – artists, editors, writers and directors – is reduced.

For example, the emphasis on creating blockbuster albums has had a major impact. An important part of the blockbuster strategy is to create the appearance of a best seller by paying huge advances and creating a star system. That results in fewer acquisition dollars available to be spent on artists who are not so well known, even though they may represent the next generation of talent in the musical world. Further, agents and lawyers, not the artists, take on important roles in the decision-making process. This shifts the emphasis from what should be tried as a new musical form to what will sell.

The emphasis on producing big-selling recordings may result in a reduction in the number and diversity of artistic voices in the media, with long-term negative consequences for the media firms that produce such works. For example, having less resources to develop new artists may well reduce the long-term financial strength of many companies. Over time, many of their blockbusters are bound to fail, and they will have few other offerings to provide profits to the firm. Further, focusing on only a small number of star performers reduces the pool of talent that the media companies need to position themselves successfully for the future.

In studies of other culture industries (Carroll, 1985; Powell, 1985), a widely accepted view is that mergers and acquisitions are a sure way to destroy a stable situation. Inevitably, when large companies take over entrepreneurial start ups, especially in knowledge- and culture-producing industries, the small firms lose their 'magic'. Soon the key personnel from the small company leave the corporate giant, often to start a new small company.

From the organizational ecology perspective noted earlier, multiformity corresponds to generalist organizations surviving in a very wide niche. These generalist firms produce and market a diverse range of musical products that dominate the Top 10. Because they control so much of the entertainment industry, the oligopolist firms are able to prevent smaller, specialist firms from surviving in popular music niches. The small firms prosper on products that are no longer pursued by large concentrated firms. As small firms make considerable inroads into the market, large firms respond by absorbing them through merger or joint venture, or by adjusting their now proven innovative or 'niche' products. In a sense, the thriving minor leagues or alternative companies represent the proving ground for the large mass market producers. The important point is that concentration and diversity are closely linked: concentration leads to a focus on narrow product lines (creative stagnation), thus creating the opportunity for new companies and entrepreneurs to pursue more diverse and experimental products. This suggests that concentration contains its own built-in liabilities. The resource-partitioning argument also considers production and consumption as interrelated. Concentration results in unexploited markets which are opportunities for small companies and specialist firms to thrive and exist in niches other than mainstream media pop music. In effect, the small labels have the role of 'pioneers', staking out new musical ground, while the majors play the role of 'settlers', taking care of business at home.

While a new group of small companies will inevitably arise to fill the spaces left by the 'majors' in various industries (which as the story goes all seem to lose some of their creative edge or 'street smarts' as they become more remote and bureaucratic), these small companies will undoubtedly require distribution through and perhaps financing from the 'majors'. As a result, one can expect the six transnationals to continue their domination of the international popular music business.

Even so, it is important to remember that irrespective of the fact that popular music is globally diffused by the transnational music companies, turning figures like Michael Jackson and Madonna into global stars or cult icons and creating a pseudo 'global village', the popularity of the music may differ from continent to continent and country to country as music takes on different roles in different cultural contexts. What is mutually common to all the geographical spaces in terms of popular music is the fact that musical tastes are not monolithic but are shaped and influenced by numerous social forces and cultural differences. The use of music in the private sphere means something very different than the use of music in the public sphere. Somewhere between the private and public sphere, the consumption of popular music may be the space, where people will continue to use music both for meaning and for pleasure in their daily lives. But that is another story waiting to be told.

Chapter 8

The Swedish example

I'm gonna get dressed for success,
Shaping me up for the big time baby,
Get dressed for success,
Shaping me up for your love.
          (Roxette, 'Dressed for Success')

Following in the footsteps of their Viking ancestors, today's Swedish pop stars are busy conquering the airwaves of the globe. The beautiful Viking ships of old have been replaced by music television and radio. Battle axes and swords replaced with well-crafted Euro-pop tunes, dance music and media friendly rock music. It all started with ABBA. Today, with artists like Roxette, Europe, Ace of Base, Dr Alban and Army of Lovers leading the invasion, Swedish pop music has finally made it big internationally. Swedish music has become an export industry. The paradox is that there are very few Swedish recording companies left that have not been taken over in some form by the transnational phonogram companies. During the past decade the transnationals have successively acquired control of the Swedish music industry. In this chapter we will examine that story.

CHANGES IN THE SWEDISH MEDIASCAPE

The period since the mid-1980s has seen dramatic changes upon the Swedish mediascape. The most dramatic are perhaps those concerning that often neglected medium, radio. Until 1989 Radio Sweden, a public service radio company jointly owned by the trade union movement, the press and the business community, had the sole broadcasting rights to the airwaves in Sweden. Radio Sweden consists of four channels, each of which aims at a particular audience. Program 1 caters to debate programmes and documentaries, while Program 2 is mostly devoted to classical music. Program 3 is an easy listening channel with lots of sports, news and of course popular music. Program 4 is the local channel, which also means lots of pop music. The period since the mid-1980s has seen the explosion of local and community radio on the airwaves. There has been a 400 per cent increase in the sheer amount of radio air-time, most of which is accounted for by the expansion of local radio. Most importantly, there has been a similar increase in the amount of popular music played over the airwaves, once again due to local and community radio which have popular music as their main programme source. The Swedish music industry initially counted their blessings over the radio boom which was prompted by the conservative coalition government making good on its pledge to open the airwaves to commercial radio. In 1993 the government sold out attractive radio frequencies in all the major cities to private organizations. The form of the sell out was by public auction, with the most attractive frequency going to the highest bidder, and so on.

The situation for television is similar although the boom in air-time has come from different sources. Sweden has two public service television channels. Channel 1 is Stockholm based, while channel 2 gathers its programmes from other districts throughout the country. In fact, it is difficult to distinguish between the two channels as both consist of a mix of Swedish programmes, foreign series and documentaries and a similar portion of sports and news. While the politicians were still debating the pros and cons of establishing a third commercial channel the cable and satellite revolution hit Sweden. In 1991 over 40 per cent of the households in Sweden had access to cable television which, depending on the area, consisted of between ten and thirty different channels, mostly foreign commercial stations. Consequently a third, commercially funded, national channel was established to compete with both the public service channels and the satellite stations. A large percentage of the programme content on the cable channels has proven to be popular music, a cheap and effective programme source. MTV Europe claims to have 2 million viewers in Sweden, which could partly explain their recent interest in Swedish bands.

At the same time, as in most other countries with commercial media systems, the music audience has become a commodity that is sold through the various media to advertisers. Audience power thus becomes synonymous with the size of audience a medium can deliver to a potential advertiser (Smythe, 1981). This is particularly interesting in a country such as Sweden that has long been free from advertising on the broadcast media but is now undergoing the transition to commercial stations funded by advertising. The Swedish public service TV channels are now regularly criticized for paying too much attention to audience size instead of programme content.

THE SWEDISH PHONOGRAM INDUSTRY

The Swedish phonogram market has been described as being relatively important from an international perspective, 'but hardly large enough for the likes and dislikes of Swedish record buyers to play any appreciable part in the decisions made by multinational record companies as to the contents of their products' (Malm, 1982: 53). In 1992, approximately $200 million worth of phonograms were sold in Sweden putting it in the top 15 countries in world sales. (That is, of those countries that belong to the IFPI and keep accurate statistics.) Of all the 11,412 phonograms released in 1992 in Sweden only 727 were by Swedish artists (Table 8.1).

Despite the overwhelming majority of foreign albums released, Swedish artists play a major role for the phonogram companies. In terms of total sales in 1992, Swedish artists accounted for 32 per cent while foreign artists had 68 per cent (Table 8.2).

The total number of Swedish phonogram companies has been estimated at somewhere between 100 and 150. The majority of these release less than ten albums per year, with many releasing only their own self-produced music. The production of phonograms in Sweden, as in many small countries, is dominated by the transnational companies. The dominating position of the transnational phonogram companies is built upon their control of the importation and distribution of phonograms. Economies of scale enable the big firms to control the market at the expense of the dozens of smaller independent labels who find it much harder and more

Table 8.1 Total releases of international/Swedish phonograms

	1986	1988	1990	1992
International releases	2,956	4,493	6,553	10,685
Swedish releases	530	670	779	727
Total releases	3,486	5,163	7,332	11,412

Source: IFPI

Table 8.2 Total sales, Swedish/foreign (%)

Origin	1986	1988	1990	1992
Swedish	30	34	32	32
Foreign	70	66	68	68
Total	100	100	100	100

Source: IFPI

costly to manufacture and distribute their own products. In Sweden, as in most other countries where the transnationals are present, the transnationals distribute not only their own phonogram releases but also those of local domestic companies. The transnationals can make money distributing domestic releases while at the same time lowering their own distribution costs. The exporting of artists from the core market to a small market such as Sweden is financially very rewarding for the parent label. For example, an American label such as Warner Music selling an American artist overseas has no manufacturing, promotional or marketing costs. All the manufacturing, marketing and promotional costs of releasing the new Madonna album are paid for by the local Warner Music branch in each country or region. The American branch of Warner Music simply supplies the master tape and marketing suggestions and makes money on the international royalties.

The remaining Swedish independent labels are organized by the Swedish Independent Music Producers group (SOM). There has also been a wave of buyouts and mergers amongst this group of independent labels. The MNW Record Group is now the biggest of the independents, controlling other indie labels, such as MVG, Amalthea and Radium. MNW has some 50 artists on their roster and has an estimated 700 albums in their back catalogue.

The distribution of phonograms in Sweden is dominated by the Association of Gramophone Suppliers (GLF) which is made up of the largest phonogram companies. Those companies affiliated to the GLF are the transnational EMI, BMG, Sony Music, Warner Music, Polygram and a scattering of small Swedish labels. The GLF has a monopoly on the distribution of phonograms in Sweden. This means that as well as distributing their own products they also make money distributing the products of smaller independent labels. Hellman (1983) notes that perhaps the most important aspect of the transnationals' distribution monopoly is that it functions as an information system, enabling them to see how demand for different types of music develops. In this way they gain valuable knowledge that they can use in developing and promoting their own artists.

In addition to the GLF there is the Music Distribution (MD) company which distributes the phonograms of the independent Swedish SOM group and foreign alternative labels. The GLF-affiliated companies have dominated sales and distribution of phonograms in Sweden throughout the 1970s and 1980s. They controlled approximately 85 per cent of total sales in 1992.

What happens in a small country such as Sweden when the transnationals stop working with local companies and open up their own branches? Sweden is an interesting example, because since the early 1980s the three largest domestic companies have been bought up or manoeuvred out of the marketplace by the transnationals. Metronome, Elektra and Sonet all survived by having a 50 per cent domestic/50 per cent foreign repertoire. They made money distributing the phonograms of the transnationals and could use the profits in the producing and selling of Swedish artists. In 1979 Metronome was sold to Warner, while in 1989 Elektra collapsed when BMG set up a branch office and terminated its distribution contract with Elektra.

The case of Sonet is particularly interesting. Until about 1989 approximately one-third of Sonet's revenues came from their licensing deals with Island, Chrysalis and Polar. Essentially this meant that Sonet distributed Island, Chrysalis and Polar material for sale in Sweden. The money made through these licensing deals provided a source of income to finance Sonet's own Swedish roster of artists. Within a twelve-month period the Swedish Polar label and the British Island label were bought up by the Dutch transnational Polygram. The British Chrysalis label was bought up by the British transnational EMI. Polygram and EMI quickly terminated the licensing deals with Sonet, who overnight had their revenues reduced by one-third. Sonet tried to compensate by producing even more Swedish artists but found it a losing cause and decided to sell out to Polygram in 1991.

In Table 8.3 the market shares in Sweden are shown for 1988, 1990 and 1992. This clearly illustrates how, through the purchase of Sonet and the collapse of Elektra, the transnationals have consolidated their hold on

Table 8.3 Phonogram market shares in Sweden

Company	Market share (%)		
	1988	1990	1992
Sony	16	16	15
EMI	16	15	20
Warner	17	18	15
Polygram	12	13	20
BMG	—	12	15
Virgin	6	7	—
Elektra	12	—	—
Sonet	7	7	—
SOM	4	4	5
Others	10	8	10
Total	100	100	100

Source: IFPI

the market. These figures are the total market shares for the sales of all phonograms by all companies in Sweden, not just hit list music. Together the transnationals have 85 per cent of the market shares, while the largest surviving Swedish SOM group has 5 per cent and the remaining companies 10 per cent.

The purchase of Polar Music (aka Sweden Music) by Polygram is also an interesting case. ABBA's record company, Polar, was originally involved in the exporting of Swedish music (ABBA) around the world. They were not involved in the selling of imported music in Sweden. Polar licensed the distributing rights to ABBA's music to different companies in different countries. They originally used the company profits to buy up several Swedish music publishers (Wallis and Malm, 1984). These publishing rights as well as Sonet's vast catalogue of Swedish popular music are now owned and controlled by Polygram's head office.

An increasing trend that Sweden shares with most phonogram-producing and -consuming nations is the concentration of sales among a small number of big sellers. For example, in 1990 a mere 30 albums accounted for approximately 25 per cent of all sales. This is not a trend that is specific only to the phonogram industry. For example, in the Swedish film industry the 10 most popular films in 1990 accounted for 43 per cent of all ticket sales. Where does all this lead us? First, the amount of popular music used on radio and television has increased immensely. Second, the transnationals are now firmly entrenched in the Swedish music business. This leads us to turn to the artists who make the music.

THE SWEDISH MUSIC SCENE

The unique thing about the Swedish group ABBA was that they were able to combine a total pastiche of musical styles together with a 'camp' style of dressing while at the same time being the first Swedish band to really look beyond the limitations of the Scandinavian market by thinking internationally. ABBA were also very much a studio entity which became obvious when one saw the number of backing musicians and singers they always took on tour. The individual members of ABBA, Björn, Benny, Agnetha and Frida, were all successful solo artists in Sweden long before winning the Eurovision Song Contest changed their lives for ever. In this sense their careers followed the traditional paths from local to national to international success that Frith (1988b) has called the 'rock' model based on a pyramid of levels that artists must climb from bottom to the top. This 'working your way up the ladder of success' model represents the traditional way of 'making it' in the music industry and is still seen

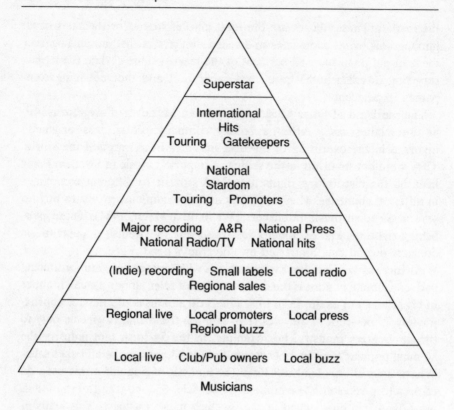

Figure 8.1 The rock

Source: Frith, 1988b

as being 'authentic' and a standard against which other career paths can be measured. Figure 8.1 represents the rock model or pyramid of career success.

The Roxette story is equally interesting. Roxette is surely one of the most successful new Euro-bands to arrive in recent years. Sales of the 1988 *Look Sharp* album are up over 8 million units, while the 1991 album *Joyride* has surpassed the 11 million mark, making it one of the biggest selling albums of that year around the world. The 1992 *Tourism* album has sold 4 million copies, while the 1994 *Crash!Boom!Bang!* album is expected to sell over 5 million copies and has thus been given the appropriate advertising budget. Still Roxette have a long way to go before reaching the hundreds of millions their Swedish predecessor ABBA sold over their 12-year-long career. While Roxette are dressed for success into the 1990s they most certainly learned their career moves from ABBA.

Roxette are now the most successful Swedish band ever in terms of chart success. They have had an unprecedented four Billboard number one singles. Contrary to public belief Roxette are not an overnight success story, but instead represent the traditional 'rock' model of career success. Singer, guitar player, song writer Per Gessle is a former 'teeny bopper' star whose band Gyllene Tider was very successful in the early 1980s. When the band broke up he turned to making solo albums. Singer Marie Fredriksson has consistently been one of the most successful and respected female solo artists in the 1980s in Sweden. Both Gessle and Fredriksson could not get any bigger in Sweden with their respective solo careers. As an experiment Gessle and Fredriksson, who grew up together in the same small town of Halmstad, decided to make an album together as a rock group singing in English. The first single, 'Neverending Love', sold 35,000 copies in Sweden during the summer of 1986. The ensuing album *Pearls of Passion* sold 280,000 copies, a gold record in Sweden. The next Roxette album *Look Sharp* came out in Sweden in 1988 on the EMI label. The album did well in Sweden and the Swedish branch office of EMI showcased the band for all the other European branches of the company in the hope that they would do a combined promotional campaign to sell the band internationally. While EMI–Europe was mildly interested in the Roxette project, EMI–America was not at all interested and passed on releasing the record in the States.

An American high school exchange student in Sweden took the album home with him and over several months pestered local disc jockeys in Minneapolis into playing Roxette. In January DJs started playing the single 'The Look' and things took off from there. It became a cult hit and radio stations started copying it and playing it as the record didn't exist in America. EMI then seized the opportunity and spent $135,000 on a new video. Two months later on 29 March 1989 'The Look' made the number one slot on the Billboard charts and an international career was assured. On 26 October 1989 the single 'Listen to Your Heart' went to number one on Billboard. In 1990 the single 'It Must Have Been Love' from the movie soundtrack to *Pretty Woman* made number one on Billboard and sold over 500,000 copies in the States alone. The first single 'Joyride' from the album of the same name went to number one on Billboard in May of 1991. In 1991 Roxette started their first ever 'world tour' as headliners.

The story of Swedish rapper Leila K is very different from that of Roxette. A first generation Swede, Leila K was discovered singing play-back at a discothèque by two DJs. They encouraged her and together they made a record for BMG in 1990. Two singles from the album, 'Got to Get' and 'Rok the Nation', both made the Top 10 in the British charts in 1990. A new Swedish artist with no previous career or Swedish following became virtually overnight a success story. Leila K in many ways represents a new model of career paths.

The success of Dr Alban is another interesting example. Dr Alban is a Nigerian who studied dentistry in Sweden. He worked in the evening as a DJ at various Stockholm discos. Like many DJs he was interested in making his own music. His first attempts were panned by the press and he was criticized for being a terrible singer. Dr Alban persisted, signed a contract with Polygram, and had some initial success on certain dance charts. An international promotion was undertaken and Dr Alban has become a star in such diverse places as Europe, South America and Asia, thanks, in part, to MTV.

Swedish pop group Ace of Base are another good example of an overnight success story. In the spring of 1994 they became the first Swedes to have both the number one single and number one album on the American Billboard charts with their single 'The Sign' from the album of the same name. The group from Gothenburg, consisting of two sisters, their brother and a friend, were essentially a basement studio project with dreams of making a record. They sent demos around the country but could not get a recording deal with a Swedish company. Nobody believed in their musical talent enough to sign them to a contract. They eventually signed with a small Danish label, Mega, who released an album in Scandinavia. Several radio stations picked up on the singles 'All That She Wants' and 'Happy Nation' and soon the videos were being played on television. Interest was shown in the international market and a new deal was signed first with the Metronome label in Germany and then BMG's Arista label in the United States. A new album was mixed and an international promotion campaign embarked upon. To date their album sales after the success in the American market have already surpassed those of Roxette.

Ace of Base sold 8 million CD albums in the USA and 15 million worldwide in 1994. Their album *The Sign* was the biggest selling album of the year on the 1994 Billboard charts as was the single of the same name. They have won awards at the Billboard Awards as well as at the American Music Awards. In November 1994 they performed live for the first time at the MTV Europe Awards broadcast from Brandenburger Tor, Berlin. Why have Ace of Base found such phenomenal success? Some claim it is because they look and sound like an ABBA groomed for the 1990s.

Another 'overnight success' story is songstress Jennifer Brown, from Gothenburg. Sweden has been bombarded with her promotional material,

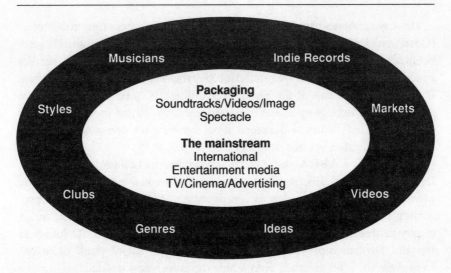

Figure 8.2 The talent pool

Source: Frith, 1988b

and she has been on the cover of most of the national music magazines. A polished album has been released, complete with some equally polished videos. The album has already gone to number one in Sweden and an international promotion is in the works. She has already shown up on the British charts and very soon could be competing in the Whitney Houston, Mariah Carey category of torch song pop music.

Stakka Bo has also had hit singles on the Euro-charts and expects to break out to a larger audience with his next release. Pandora, Atomic Swing and Clawfinger have also had success outside Sweden. The latest success story, at the time of writing, is the country/techno! group, Rednex, with their dance floor version of the old standard 'Cotton Eye Joe'.

This second or new model of how careers now work has been called the 'talent pool' by Frith (1988b). The rise of music television and the video selling of new pop artists have opened new career paths. The dynamics involved in the talent pool work from the centre outwards. Frith (1988b: 113) explains that, 'there are no longer gatekeepers regulating the flow of stardom, but multinationals "fishing" for material, pulling ideas, sounds, styles, performers from the talent pool and dressing them up for worldwide consumption'. The process is most certainly more irrational than the 'rock model' as 'going fishing' is certainly a riskier business than grooming an artist or band. Figure 8.2 represents the 'talent pool' model of career development.

The transnationals try to cut the risk by maintaining a large 'repertoire' (Garnham, 1987) of artists and cultural products to choose from. This has been one of their ways of dealing with the fact that they can't predict which of their artists will be purchased by which segment of the audience. It is this 'dictatorship of the public' (Hennion, 1983) or fear of an active audience that both propels the musical industry forward in search of new styles and artists while at the same time ensuring the constant reworking of already familiar sounds and faces.

The stories of ABBA and Roxette compared to Leila K, Ace of Base, Dr Alban, Stakka Bo, Rednex and Jennifer Brown represent in many ways the two different models of career paths – ABBA and Roxette representing the traditional model or 'rock' of gradual growth over the years of paying dues; Leila K, Ace of Base, Dr Alban, Stakka Bo, Rednex and Jennifer Brown, representing the new model or 'talent pool' of artists from which the phonogram companies dip into when needed.

The transnationals have been doing a lot of 'fishing' in Sweden in recent years. BMG has released records by rapper/toaster Papa Dee and by soul/pop songstress Titiyo. The former has worked the club scene for a number of years, the latter a relative newcomer as a solo artist, though a seasoned backup singer. Sony has released three albums by the melodic hard rock band, Europe, and had an enormous success with their song 'The Final Countdown' in the international marketplace. Polygram has had success with the 'camp' pop band Army of Lovers, which is in essence a studio band complete with two fashion models that mostly 'perform' in the videos. In fact Army of Lovers' only stage performance to date has been as models for avant-garde designer Jean-Paul Gaultier's fashion line in Paris. The perfect product for the 1990s video age perhaps, no expensive tours, no band to underwrite and certainly no musical differences.

What is striking about all the above mentioned artists is that they all sing in English and are aiming at breaking into the international market. This is a stance that is taken for granted among many younger Swedish artists who see an international career as a logical possibility and a normal progression in the age of MTV's *global jukebox*. Also important to note is that most of these artists were originally signed to Swedish labels but have ended up as a result of company takeovers with the various transnationals. Perhaps we need to add 'poaching' alongside our 'fishing' allegory.

At the same time, the transnationals are not averse to putting out the music of artists who sing in Swedish. BMG had the biggest selling album in Sweden in 1990 with soft rocker Tomas Ledin. Sony/CBS has always done well with Magnus Uggla, a clever pop artist who only sings in

Swedish. Likewise, Polygram and more recently BMG have had substantial commercial success with Carola who has been one of Sweden's most popular female pop singers throughout the 1980s. In terms of the 'rock' versus the 'talent pool' models of development one can quite clearly say that most Swedish artists who sing only in Swedish have and still are following the traditional 'rock' model of advancement. This could change in the future as Swedish television has started producing a weekly Video Top Twenty for Swedish artists only, thus opening up the possibility for local 'overnight' success stories.

In trying to explain the sudden success of Swedish musicians in the international market several informants have commented upon and compared it to the Björn Borg effect for tennis in Sweden. The success of Borg inspired others, like Mats Wilander and Stefan Edberg, on to success. The same situation is perhaps at work in music, with the phenomenal success of ABBA, Europe and Roxette inspiring other younger musicians to aim for the international market. Another important explanation is certainly the fact that a high percentage of Swedish children attend community music schools where they learn to sing and play an instrument. A further reason is simply that Swedes are good at copying styles and reworking music into something new.

OPEN PRODUCTION SYSTEM

Due to the ever increasing range of music styles the transnationals have opted for a more 'open' system of production. This process is at work in Sweden as in most other countries. Multiple independent production units take care of A&R and recording, while the 'mother' company takes care of manufacturing, marketing and distribution. This enables the transnationals to exploit both the talent of small creative units to identify potential successful new artists and sounds, as well as the advantages of large-scale manufacturing and distribution. In effect, the modern transnational phonogram company consists of many independently operating creative units at the 'input' side, and concentrated manufacturing and distribution at the 'output' side. To regulate the flow of products through the channels of a transnational, an internal market is at work, in which the independent units act like they would in a more normal market. For example, Sony USA and Sony UK are in competition to have their products released in Sweden. This system of internal competition is coupled with a centralized control set-up that helps the local units to best deploy their resources. All creative units, at a national level, are allowed to try out new products, artists and ideas within their budget. Once a particular act becomes successful in either a geographical region, or within a specialized music genre, the combined resources are provided. That particular artist becomes a priority. As a consequence, the national units can concentrate their resources on this potentially successful artist, thereby increasing the chances of turning a local success into an international one.

An example of this open production system is the Polygram International-funded label Stockholm Records. Polygram owns 50 per cent in this joint venture to create 'Sweden's first and only International label' for the sole purpose of producing artists for the international market. Stockholm Records has its production units broken down into 'project teams' that work with every artist. A company executive stated that, 'Our most important decision was to leave the administration to Polygram ... Our model builds on production and creativity instead.'

Stockholm Records is especially concerned with the visual image of their artists so naturally one of the most important roles is played by the 'stylist' who works on the artists' choice of clothes, hairstyle and general attitude in videos, and live performances and interviews. An Army of Lovers spokesman stated that, 'There has been a sudden interest in Scandinavia at the same time that companies are looking beyond England and the USA ... you have to be original and look exciting ... it has to be visual to function internationally.' Consequently, Army of Lovers' stylist is considered so important that she gets credit as a member of the band.

In 1994 MCA opened a branch in Sweden. They intend to look after sales and promotions themselves, but have signed a five-year deal with BMG for distribution within Sweden. Parallel with the Swedish office, MCA has opened offices in Denmark, Norway, Belgium, France, Holland, Italy and Spain. The head Euro-office is situated in London. MCA artists such as Aerosmith, Guns 'n' Roses and Nirvana are no strangers to Swedish fans. MCA has also stated their interest in eventually signing Swedish artists to recording contracts.

In the words of MCA music president Al Teller:

For all the obvious reasons, ultimately MCA will have to participate in domestic repertoire throughout the world ... Right now, fundamentally we are dependent on the English language for our product. We don't enjoy the benefits of local artists selling enormous quantities of records in their territories. To be competitive with the other worldwide majors at some point we have to tap into local repertoire. That is certainly an important item on our agenda as we look out into the future internationally.

(quoted in Rutten, 1991: 297)

These remarks are echoed by a BMG executive who outlined the company's policy as an effort to 'regionalise local repertoire and, in some cases, to globalise local repertoire'.

The following EMI Europe executive gets right to the point:

My job is to make as much money as possible for EMI. We have to have a well oiled machine that can quickly get the products out there with good marketing. At the end of the day the company shareholders want a return on their investment and the consumers want to buy products as cheaply as possible.

This philosophy is put into practice by a Polygram A&R man:

Music is a high risk business ... the goal is to make more money than it costs to produce the album ... Selling music is like selling fish sticks or hamburgers, the package, the image, has to correspond to the product, otherwise the customer feels cheated ... Two singles ... two hits that we can work with ... if they can't give me two singles then they may as well lie down and die ... To sell a band internationally you have to give the foreign public something they haven't had before.

The dream for this and many A&R executives is to take an artist from national to international success. This happens quite rarely, partially because promoting an act internationally is a very costly undertaking. Not many artists have the talent or the willpower and stamina needed. First of all the artist as a rule must have had some major success in the domestic market. Then somebody in the record company must believe strongly enough in the artist that they are willing to start all over again with an international marketing campaign. Of course not all artists are interested in an international career. An established artist that is at the top of the popularity pyramid at home is not necessarily interested in starting at the bottom of the heap again as an unknown. Especially when the international marketing process usually involves eating a certain amount of humble pie, taking orders from strangers, doing endless interviews, taking part in publicity blitzes and playing playback lip-synched performances on variety television programmes in foreign countries.

Each of the transnationals have approximately 200 artists on their European rosters. That is to say, for example, that EMI has 200 European artists when all the domestic artists in each European country are added up and accounted for. It is the local national offices that have the responsibility of marketing their own artists. Naturally very few domestic artists are afforded the benefits of an international marketing campaign.

The role of the transnational music companies in Sweden is now predominantly concerned with three major activities.

1 To ensure the local selling of international artists (a job previously licensed to Swedish companies).
2 To ensure the local selling of local artists (a job previously done by Swedish companies).
3 Increasingly important is to develop local artists to plug into the international 'talent pool' (a job nobody did until recently).

Thus the transnationals have not merely used their stronger position to concentrate on importing international hit music by foreign superstars. The transnationals need to continually seek new talent combined with the existence of a demand for a number of national stars in domestic markets. Often this new talent is in the form of artists who have established themselves first through smaller independent companies.

The successful national artists play an important role in offsetting the risks that go with superstar dependence for major transnationals (see Wallis and Malm, 1992). The transnationals' income from sales of Swedish phonograms ranges from between about 25 to 35 per cent. For example, the Swedish soft rocker Tomas Ledin sold 500,000 phonograms for BMG's Swedish label, The Record Station, in Sweden, in 1990/91. That in a country with a population of under nine million!

The Anglo-American dominance in popular music appears to be on the decline in Sweden. The rise of 'world music' has coincided with a similar rise of non-Anglo-American artists making their way into the elite division of the international pop music 'talent pool'. As a case in point, one can look to the export of Swedish popular music which has increased substantially in recent years (Table 8.4). The collection of royalties, mostly performance rights for Swedish music played in other countries, has gone up 300 per cent over the past decade, according to STIM, the national collection agency.

The best known export example are Roxette who have sold an estimated 25 million records to date for EMI. Roxette were marketed and made it big in the USA before they became popular in Europe. More recent

Table 8.4 Swedish artists' foreign performance royalty income (live and media, $ million)

1990	1991	1992	1993
5.3	5.9	7.1	9.4

Source: STIM

successful Swedish exports such as Dr Alban, Army of Lovers and Ace of Base were all promoted successfully on the pan-European market first before taking the leap over the Atlantic. Important to be aware of in this case is the tension involved between transnational record company executives in the different countries. Getting a Swedish artist released in Germany or Italy often means promising to release a German or Italian artist in Sweden. For a Swedish artist on an independent label the chance of getting a record released in any foreign markets is virtually non-existent, although there does exist a company, Export Music Sweden, that specializes in promoting independent labels in foreign markets.

National charts also become problematic. Whose music are we measuring when a Swedish artist is released by a transnational? As noted earlier, phonogram sales are becoming less relevant. It has been pointed out that small national markets now serve as 'test markets' which the transnationals use as information networks in deciding which artists to release in different countries (Burnett, 1992a; Frith, 1991). One thing the sales charts are still good for is comparing what is selling in different countries. Examining the Euro-charts in 1994 reveals that the charts in Sweden have much more in common with its nearest European neighbours than with the southern European or American charts. Simply stated, regional differences remain.

A straight analysis of the sales charts in Sweden for the first week of April 1994 reveals some interesting statistics. For example we find that 10 songs or 50 per cent of the Top 20 chart were by Swedish artists. The remaining 10 were American, British and Dutch. Of the 10 Swedish songs 4 or 40 per cent were sung in Swedish, the remaining 6 in English as were all the songs by foreign artists. Only 2 songs on the chart were released by independent companies, all the rest by transnationals. Musical styles ranged from, pop, rock, soul, dance, rap and heavy metal.

But the important point to be made is that the sales charts are no longer the best indicator of what people are actually listening to, they simply reflect the number of phonograms bought, not what people are listening to on the radio, on TV and in live music situations. Ronny and Ragge, 1993's overnight sensation in Sweden, are a case in point. Ronny and Ragge are two young comedians who have appeared on various Swedish TV shows for the past couple of years doing an act where they portray two greaseballs from the countryside who end up in the big city. Some of the sketches involved music so in the early spring 1993 they released an album aptly entitled *Let's Screw (Let's Pök)*. To date, the album has sold over 100,000 copies which in Sweden makes it a platinum album! But the album has sold slowly making very little impact on the Top 20 charts!

In the summer of 1993 they played the lucrative outdoor parks concert circuit where they did a total of 35 concerts to an estimated audience of 150,000. They were played constantly on the radio, continue to appear on TV and are written about in all the teen magazines. Ronny and Ragge were simply 'this year's model' in Sweden in 1993, who will make absolutely no impact in any other country, but will be a dominant factor in the musical life of some Swedish youth. They are in effect 'local heroes'.

If communication and cultural studies have taught us anything in the past decade it is that the public aren't 'passive cultural dopes', but are busy in their interaction with the various media. The Swedish public continues to often choose its own musicians, films and TV series over foreign material. With an expanding media sector, a shift to narrowcasting formats, and increasingly 'nomadic' audiences, it remains likely that music lovers will continue to support their local heroes while still enjoying their international superstars.

CONCLUSION

What conclusions can we draw and what questions can we raise about the place of Swedish music in the impending new economic formation of Europe? First one must question what is specifically Swedish about Swedish popular music other than language? Swedish musicians, like musicians anywhere, have for a number of years usually been looking to the west for new influences and sources of inspiration. These influences have in turn produced everything from pure copycat bands and sounds to interesting and even unique Swedish sounds. The language has in many ways acted as a 'cultural screen'. Swedish rap music certainly sounds strange to foreign ears but it is popular and certainly meaningful to those youth in the high density residential areas that choose to listen to it!

There are no official quotas on the amount of Swedish music that must be played on the radio although traditionally it has been around 30 per cent. With the continuing deregulation of the Swedish airwaves this might very well change. One can foresee a debate about this in the future as the Swedish radio listener begins to experience things like 'narrowcasting' and 'segmentation' on a regular basis. It will be interesting to see what sort of radio formats will thrive and which will perish from the new media soundscape. Already the Swedish phonogram industry executives are complaining that all the new commercial radio stations sound alike, only playing Phil Collins and Elton John.

Swedish musicians who perform in Swedish will probably continue to do well in Sweden and in the other Nordic countries as they have traditionally always done. Economic changes in the south will not change that. One can foresee the possibility of more and more artists making phonograms in both Swedish and English aimed at different markets. In fact this has already started to happen.

The transfer of power in the Swedish music industry to the trans-nationals could have very real consequences. Older musicians have complained that the decision-making process will become more complicated and that direct contact between musician and phonogram company will diminish. Younger musicians on the other hand see mostly positive opportunities to get their music out into the rest of Europe and possibly the world. The age or generation differences seem to play a larger role than one's political colours in this question. The one point that everyone agrees upon is that the transnationals' ownership and control of almost the entire back catalogue of Swedish popular music is not a good thing. The consequences of this change in ownership have yet to be seen, but the issues raised are similar to those being raised in the United States over the partial Japanese takeover of the film and music industries. One can assume that the selling of a cultural heritage is not popular anywhere.

The paradox is that at the same time that the phonogram industry is once again in a period of high market concentration and the transnationals have taken control of the Swedish marketplace it is easier than ever for the Swedish public to come in contact with new musics. The technological expansion of radio and television channels has seen to that. One can argue that the 'fishing trips' the transnationals and the small independents have done in places like Scandinavia, Africa and South America combined with the rereleases of entire back catalogues of older artists has produced a repertoire of music styles without precedent in the long history of recorded popular music.

Chapter 9

Future sounds: a global jukebox?

> One Planet, One Music.
> (MTV advert)

A technical revolution is happening in the area of interactive multimedia systems that will have far reaching consequences for the international music industry. Essentially the equivalent of software for cable television, these new systems are combining the computing and television worlds to radically alter the way popular culture is delivered. Time Warner, the largest entertainment company, Tele-Communications Inc., the largest cable TV company, and Microsoft, the largest computer software company, have formed a joint venture tentatively called Cablesoft. Together they will develop systems for the digital distribution of entertainment and information into the home. Cable subscribers will be able to pick and choose from the vast Time Warner archive of music, films and television shows. The companies hope the new venture will lead the way in establishing a standard for the transmission of the coming generation of interactive programmes.

Media giant Time Warner also plans to launch a fifth American TV network. This would of course pose a serious threat to America's existing national giants, ABC, CBS, NBC and the smaller FOX. This comes at a time when media companies are scrambling to take advantage of the fast growing trend towards multimedia entertainment, in which television and other services are brought into homes through combined phone and cable networks. Time Warner is a strong competitor; it owns one of Hollywood's biggest movie studios, and is the top supplier of TV programmes to the existing networks, producing 26 prime time series. It operates the second largest cable network in the United States and owns the Home Box Office pay-TV network. It also has powerful music and publishing divisions to provide additional software. The big three networks have seen their market share halved since the 1970s and now control just

45 per cent of the US television industry. The networks have lost their market share to cable television programmes, to satellite TV, to the FOX network and to the independent stations built around the booming syndication market.

Time Warner Entertainment (TWE) which is comprised of the Warner Brothers movie studio, the Home Box Office pay-TV cable channel and Time Warner's cable businesses is controlled by the parent Time Warner company which owns 63 per cent. Time Warner sold 25 per cent of TWE in 1993 to telecommunications giant US West for $2.5 billion. Time Warner had previously sold 12 per cent of TWE to the Japanese electronics firm Toshiba and trading company Itochu for $1 billion in 1991. Gerald Levin, CEO of Time Warner, and Richard McCormick, CEO of US West, in a joint statement announcing the deal, said:

> As the telecommunications marketplace becomes increasingly competitive, the strategic partnership of TWE, whose partners include Time Warner, US West, Toshiba and Itochu, is designed to accelerate the construction and operation of networks that will provide instantaneous transmission of limitless information, telephony, and entertainment options for our customers.
>
> (*Clarinews*, 15 September 1993)

Time Warner has also announced plans to create an interactive news-on-demand service in which customers will be able to choose and control the content, length and order of news programming. Gerald Levin, CEO of Time Warner, said:

> Our news-on-demand service will be a significant product of the Full Service Network, joining other services – movies-on-demand, video games, interactive catalogue shopping and telephony services – offering previously unavailable levels of convenience, choice and control to those who subscribe to the Full Service Network.
>
> (*Clarinews*, 16 November 1993)

The new service will include local, world and national news, business and finance, sports, reviews, health news and weather.

At stake is control of the unobtrusive cable box that connects many television sets. That box has become a battleground for computer, telephone and cable companies. As an industry executive explained:

> this has tremendous economic and social importance; it is the gateway for popular culture; this is the substitute for newspapers and magazines and catalogues and movies, and that gives it enormous economic potential for those who control the gateway.

MTV's parent company Viacom, together with AT&T, is developing an interactive television system that will allow viewers to communicate direct with MTV. This means choosing what videos one wants to see as well as ordering information on the artist and record via text-TV. The multimedia archive will also enable one to choose songs to hear on the radio, films to see on the television and video games to play on the screen.

Paramount Communications is also working with AT&T on interactive television programming. The programmes are being designed for delivery over cable TV systems, telephone lines or satellite links. Analysts believe that despite formidable technical obstacles, interactive TV may be in as many as 40 million US homes by the year 2000. The presence of AT&T in the interactive market may help the technology become available on a mass market basis more quickly than previously forecast.

The merger of Paramount Communications and Viacom created a multimedia giant that plans to expand aggressively to compete on equal footing with Time Warner, Sony and News Corporation. The estimated $10 billion deal is the largest media industry merger since the 1989 marriage that created Time Warner.

Viacom is a diversified entertainment and communications company with operations in four principal segments: cable television, broadcasting, networks and entertainment. Paramount is involved in the entertainment and publishing businesses. Through its subsidiaries, Paramount Pictures and Madison Square Gardens, it produces and distributes feature films, TV shows, home videos, and operates theatres.

'The possibilities are unlimited', said Paramount CEO Martin Davis at a press conference. 'We are both opportunistic and we will be more so.' Viacom CEO Sumner Redstone commented: 'there are all kinds of opportunities and all kinds of the word I hate – synergies'. Both executives said they expect the new company to invest heavily in booming interactive technologies, designed to bring a smorgasbord of services and 500 channels of TV into homes. Redstone said the key capability of the merged company will be its ability to produce film, TV programmes, books and music and to distribute them. He noted that MTV is already in 240 million homes worldwide and that 'software is the name of the game, what separates companies is their ability to do software' (Clarinews, 13 September 1993).

Sony Music, Blockbuster Entertainment and Pace Entertainment are involved in a joint venture to develop and operate musical concert amphitheatres. The development mixes the music industry muscle of Sony, which has an extensive array of recording artists, with the marketing savvy of Blockbuster, king of home video retailing. This development also underscores the growing consolidation within the entertainment industry. Blockbuster has been extremly aggressive since 1992 about expanding its operations into new entertainment ventures, anticipating its home video stores will become obsolete in their present form. Wayne Huizenga, CEO of Blockbuster, said: 'Blockbuster Entertainment's vision is to present the widest possible range of entertainment to the widest possible audience' (*Clarinews*, 13 September 1993). Blockbuster has been on a buying binge in the 1990s. It bought 270 record stores and 160 video stores for $150 million from Philips Electronics. They spent $165 million to acquire nearly half of TV production concern Spelling Entertainment Group. It also acquired record retailers Music Plus and Sound Warehouse for $125 million, and formed a $150 million partnership with Britain's Virgin Group for a chain of 'megastores' in the United States and Europe. It has also formed joint ventures with International Business Machines (IBM) to deliver music, films and games electronically to retailers and is considering starting up a cable TV superstation.

At the time of the deal (November 1993) Thomas Mottola, CEO of Sony Music Entertainment, said: 'The opportunity to develop projects with Blockbuster Entertainment is both exciting and promising. Together we can expand each other's entertainment capabilities and present great performers, in venues that will best showcase their talents, to audiences around the world' (ibid.).

Media mogul Rupert Murdoch, moving to take advantage of sweeping technological advances, has also announced plans to expand his global communications empire by uniting his SKY Television network in part-nerships with other major communications companies. Murdoch said the moves were a result of the 'confusing, frightening and breathtakingly exciting' revolution in communications technology and would mean 'jobs, jobs, jobs' for the British economy (*Clarinews*, 2 September 1993). Speaking to an audience of British industrial and political leaders, Murdoch said his organization, the News Corporation, would enter into a partnership with British Telecom to develop new ways of sending infor-mation, pictures and sound over telephone lines. Murdoch said the potential partnership will allow the two companies to explore ways of using the phone lines to deliver news, financial information and enter-tainment to every house with a telephone.

Bertelsmann Music Group has announced a new music label for CD-ROMs as part of its expansion into the booming multimedia market. The label will be the recording industry's first interactive music label. They plan to sell interactive CD-ROMs, which are high capacity compact discs combining video, text and graphics. They will give purchasers an improved music video allowing them to choose the orchestration for songs, attach a variety of images and read the lyrics. Bertelsmann has also confirmed it is seeking to make a major investment in a Hollywood film studio under a plan to expand its television operations. Bertelsmann has also said it wants to expand in eastern Europe in book clubs, TV and music, and in Asia mainly through music.

Metro-Goldwyn-Mayer has signed a distribution agreement with Polygram Filmed Entertainment. The agreement calls for MGM to distribute up to four major release Polygram films annually – meaning films that will open on at least 1,000 screens. The agreement with the Dutch media giant will help MGM improve its distribution service. The films in the deal will be produced by Polygram's Propaganda Films, Working Titles, A&M and Manifesto units. Propaganda Films produced David Lynch's *Wild at Heart* as well as TV's *Twin Peaks* (also by Lynch) and *Beverly Hills 90210*. Propaganda also produces commercials, with Nike and Pepsi being two of its largest contracts. They produce approximately 35 commercials per year as well as 125 music videos per annum.

Scandinavian Broadcasting Systems has reached an agreement with Capital Cities/ABC in which Capital Cities will acquire a 21 per cent share of the broadcaster. 'This is a strategic ownership alliance with one of the finest broadcasters in the world', said Harry Evans Sloan, CEO of SBS. 'Capital Cities/ABC has long been recognized for their innovative and pioneering spirit in establishing broadcasting and cable programming entities in the United States and throughout the world. There is no doubt that they will be of great assistance to us as we at SBS continue to establish our presence in the emerging broadcasting marketplace in Scandinavia', said Sloan. Daniel Burke, CEO, Capital Cities/ABC, said, 'This investment is another important building block in our plans to be a long-term player of consequence in the global arena. We continue to see these kinds of international partnerships as an important avenue of growth for the company' (*Clarinews*, 16 November 1993).

The proposed blockbuster $21 billion merger between Tele-Communication Inc. (TCI) and Bell Atlantic Corporation raises the perhaps most important competitive issue, which is the market for information 'content' as opposed to information 'conduit' services. Currently the cable television industry is allowed to own both the 'content' and the 'conduit' for cable services. The result has been attempts by the large cable companies, particularly Time Warner and TCI, to exert their monopolistic control over local franchise services (the conduit) to obtain monopolistic control over cable programming channels (the content). If denied access to the conduit by a cable system's owner, cable network programmers cannot achieve the 'critical mass' of viewers needed to attract national advertising or a sufficient number of subscribers required to make the network viable. Ralph Nader (1993) observes that: 'Competition in content markets should be a paramount concern of policy makers, since our society depends on a diversity of expression and the freest exchange of ideas.'

The software suppliers can be divided into two categories: the *computer software* companies like Microsoft and the *media software* companies like the Hollywood studios or the Los Angeles-based music industry. The American software has until recently dominated world markets. The idea of linking the hardware and software industries through 'information super highways' is the latest in a long line of post-industrial strategies. These information highways will be high capacity, broadband fibre-optic network connections linking together the world's computers, from personal to super. The information highway will one day provide an information age equivalent to the railroads and the highways.

Specifically what these information highways will carry, how they will be controlled and to which technical standards they will be interconnected, remains to be seen. There is also the question of whether it will be governments or the market that will impose such a future infrastructure.

While, at the time of writing, the 'information super highways' seem to be mostly in the planning stages there is already a good deal of activity going on in the United States around the somewhat smaller-scale 'electronic information highway' systems. For example, the multimedia distribution channels being set up by Time Warner and the US West telephone and cable company are going to make it extremely easy to distribute music, video and textual data via wide low-cost channels. This medium is going to allow people from their own home to query any media item they choose. They will be able to sample the item, and search for it from any number of directions.

An interesting question to raise is what will turn out to be more important, the control of the distribution channels or the control/ownership of the contents/software? The media conglomerates are certainly moving to cover both areas and legislate aspects of it. Obviously alternative media outlets have a vested interest in trying to obtain a foothold on the 'electronic highway'. Some interesting features arise here that are linked to the properties of the technology itself. If the key aspect of the technology is the ability to access resources across time and space, then the key social issue is the individual and community right to access the resources. It may turn out that rather than concentrating on how to get the alternative/ independent producers onto the highway so they can distribute their products, it may make more sense to concentrate on how to get the users in a position to access large and small resource sites. In essence, it may be more important to organize the consumers rather than the alternative producers.

The electronic highway user will soon access the resource from anywhere, be that home, office, community centre or library. Theoretically a small group of users spread out geographically can generate effective demand to sustain the product of small independent producers (entertainment or information). The potentially radical element here is that organizing the users makes sense, is easily done by the technology, and shifts effective power away from the media conglomerates and towards end users. The media giants think that the new technologies that they have invested in so heavily will consolidate the power of the traditional mass media. The point to be made is that there is the distinct possibility that the technology will have results quite the opposite of those expected by the media moguls.

THE FUTURE

The continued transnationalization is generally expected to result in the emergence or survival of roughly a half dozen mega media giants who will dominate the global market by the turn of the century.

Considering the number of recent deals and mergers among media companies there seems to be a rationale based on the old belief that bigger is better. Do cross-media mergers always make sense? Time Warner looked promising in theory. Time's magazines and cable television companies would be the distributors and popularizers of the stars generated by Warner's film and record companies. The various parts of the company were to strive for the elusive benefits of synergy. In fact, sources claim that the operations of both companies remain distinct and, so far, the merger shows little benefits.

The most fundamental of questions also need to be raised: Who's going to buy this stuff? Why? When? How much will they pay? Since the risks are high and the territory uncharted, companies all over the globe are racing into strategic alliances and joint ventures to spread their costs and risks. A research and development executive commented that, 'Right now, the industry is throwing lots of things against the wall ... what will stick isn't clear.'

One scenario sees the consumer at the home computer as becoming the ultimate programmer, creating personal menus of choices from a vast array of entertainment and information possibilities. Hand in hand with this trend is the increase in channels aimed at specific individuals and special interest groups through the strategy of narrowcasting as opposed to yesterday's broadcasting of lowest common denominator entertainment.

As journalist Gottlieb has suggested:

> Today's record companies will have to learn how to do something more sophisticated than making and distributing physical objects. They will increasingly need to market and sell information in the form of music, which is not quite the same thing. Today's passive audiences will be able to take more of the music business into their own hands, and there are increasingly signs that they want to do so. They will be able to make recordings at home (from digital radio and other things) which are indistinguishable from what they can buy in shops today; or they will have customised recordings made for them in the descendants of today's record shops. They are already straining to do more with the music than just play back someone else's performance exactly as it was recorded in a studio.
>
> (Gottlieb, 1991: 4)

This means that the record companies will have to become more like the music publishers of old, making their money from facilitating and licensing the recording and performance of music. We are already seeing a pronounced shift of phonogram company income from primary (selling of phonograms) to secondary sources (collection of publishing and performing rights). The old music business of selling packages of music to relatively passive consumers will remain a large business for quite some time. The point is that a very different sort of music business is growing up along side it.

The increase in 'user friendly' interactive multimedia systems should have profound changes on the music industry. Remember that music video has become a standard marketing and promotional tool, with the result being that the phonogram industry and television have developed a relationship similar to that between the phonogram industry and radio, one of symbiosis.

The transnational music labels have complained for several years that many of their new acts weren't getting played on MTV. Rival music companies, Warner, Sony, EMI, Polygram and BMG, have agreed to start up their own music TV channel in 1995 to rival MTV. It is too early to tell if their intent is to control the flow of content and create a channel where they get the first window on videos. Obviously the music labels want the best exposure for their artists and if MTV is no longer seen as the answer, then the primary suppliers of videos are about to go into the same business.

One of the most controversial of Viacom's many plans is its possible move into the record business and its effect on MTV. According to CEO Redstone, Viacom's policy was to stay out of the record business, so as not to compete with its suppliers. The rules have changed. Redstone said: 'Now that record companies have started to compete with us we will consider owning our own record company. There's a lot of talent out there that has attributed their success to MTV. It's a good business and we would certainly be pretty expert at it' (*European*, 21 October 1994).

The most important development of all may well turn out to be the *Internet*. Among many other functions what the Internet provides is a radical new approach to distributing music and video. Take as an example the case of Cerberus, a London-based technology company that has already demonstrated what it calls the Digital Jukebox – a system distributing CD-quality music to homes using telephone lines. The consumer, using a home computer with access to the Internet, and with some simple software, will be able to download music from the Cerberus music archive at a relatively inexpensive cost. These 'music on demand' systems are obviously a threat to the music industry's traditional distributors. Systems like the Digital Jukebox challenge the traditional distribution, marketing and spin off industries that flow from the transnational music companies to the consumer. They could render obsolete recording studios, publishers and manufacturers, even record stores – thereby taking a huge chunk out of a market that indirectly feeds the transnationals.

The problem that needs to be solved is 'who gets the royalties'. Any digital jukebox will have to sort out who gets the revenue, how it's collected and how sales can be properly audited, before they can legally distribute copyrighted music over the Internet. The transnationals are not prone to, as one executive wryly noted, 'giving away our products for free'. What is already happening is that groups like Cerberus and the Internet Underground Music Archive (IUMA) are already inviting artists to send in digital tape recordings which are then uploaded onto a database of digital music for free – it then becomes just a case of users downloading the music into their computers and playing the tracks.

Other novelties include Ringo, developed at MIT, which is a free Net-based 'personal music recommendation service', which rates music based on your tastes. When you send e-mail to Ringo, it replies with a list of musicians and groups for you to rate from 1 to 7. Evaluating this info and data, culled from users with similar tastes, Ringo recommends artists and tells you whom to avoid.

A commercial retail company CD NOW bills itself as the Internet Music Store where one can find over 140,000 CDs, cassettes and mini discs, along with ratings, reviews and biographies. The company slogan 'music for the masses' alludes to the claim that CD NOW has every album under the sun for fast delivery at low prices. CD NOW can be reached by Telnet or by checking out their World Wide Web (WWW) server, certainly a sign of things to come.

Another development sees artists increasingly using the Internet as a launching pad for a new product. YELLO recently previewed their tenth studio album *Zebra* on the Internet via their own World Wide Web page. The YELLO WWW site is a multimedia tour containing music samples, photographs, cartoons, music videos and tour information. (See the Appendix for WWW Internet music sites.)

The Internet Underground Music Archive (IUMA) is a World Wide Web (WWW) site dedicated to a particular vision based upon:

1 movement towards equal distribution for all musicians;
2 removing more of the barriers which currently keep musicians and their audience separated;
3 exposing yet more people to the Internet's vast resources, specifically relating to the electronic distribution of music.

Many Internet surfers were shocked to find Warner Brothers Records on IUMA in late 1994. The IUMA explained their decision to help Warner Brothers as follows:

> In order to create a level playing field which gives equal distribution to all artists ranging from an angsty 6th grader in his/her garage to huge mega-pop-stars, all artists must be placed side by side. The playing field cannot be even unless everyone is playing on it.

They developed their argument further by claiming:

> Warner Bros. Records' decision to make excerpts of upcoming singles available online to the entire world for free along with images and album information is a great service towards enhancing the flow of information about their musicians to their respective audience. Warner Bros. Records is now joining the IUMA family of labels working to remove the artist-to-audience barriers by allowing listeners to directly sample new music from their own homes and offices. IUMA will continue to offer and expand this service for all unsigned musicians, independent labels, and major labels who should desire it.

By the end of 1994 the IUMA contained digitalized songs by over 500 bands, most unsigned. It takes a few minutes to download a 15 second excerpt of a song and then decide if one wants to take the time (15 to 20 minutes) to download the entire song.

It is exciting that an artist anywhere can record a song at home using a Macintosh-based digital recording studio, and then put the finished song out on the Internet where it can be downloaded and listened to by a potential audience of millions.

A music technology developer noted that:

> Musicians should seize the opportunity that this kind of inexpensive recording equipment allows to make things ... The control that these bigger entities have been able to exert on musicians is disintegrating. Now if you could just get around distribution, which the major labels still control, you could completely democratize the production and distribution of music.
>
> (*Wired*, 1994b)

It should be obvious to all that developing technology that helps lots of people create music is a good thing. People stand to gain a lot through demystification of personal artistic expression. In a probable future scenario filled with endless bad media content, with too much supply and very specific demand, music might very well become devalued. But then why shouldn't the creation of music be possible for everyone who is interested? Isn't that what Attali meant by the fourth stage of musical development, that of 'composition', which foresees a new way of doing music ... Doing music for the sake of doing!

The interesting paradox is that while the six transnationals have the money and the technology to continue to dominate the production and distribution of popular music for many years to come, the digitalization of music could give them even more control and larger profits, or it could open a Pandora's box that could ultimately destroy their own control of popular music. If the electronic, digital delivery through the Internet or cable TV becomes the dominant form of music distribution in the future, then any band will be able to distribute their music themselves, directly to their fans over the wire. If artists start self-distribution over the wire then what happens to the Big Six? The music business may well never be the same. The one thing that we can be sure of (with apologies to BTO) is that 'we ain't seen nothing yet'.

Postscript

One of the things that is exciting and often frustrating about studying the entertainment industry is that things are always happening. It's hard for anyone to always be up to date. Deals are being made, mergers are being planned, new cultural products are being hyped. The summer of 1995 was certainly no exception with several major deals being made that have major consequences for the entire music industry.

First, rumours were rampant that Matsushita was tired of the entertainment business and was trying to sell MCA Movies and MCA Music Entertainment. Polygram made a secret bid but were beaten out by the Seagram Company, the Canadian liquor manufacturer! Seagram's have since stated that they are interested in acquiring more media-related holdings.

Second, the George Michael vs Sony Music conflict was resolved with Michael winning his freedom. Essentially Sony released Michael from his recording contract to sign with DreamWorks SKG and Virgin Music, in return for a $40 million release fee. DreamWorks is the newly founded entertainment company started jointly by music mogul David Geffen, movie director Steven Spielberg and movie producer Jeffery Katzenberg. The deal could be good for all the concerned parties. Sony gets cash and the right to release a greatest hits package, Michael gets a cash advance and can start making records again, the lifeblood of any artist. The big winner could be DreamWorks who get a highly successful artist to launch their new label. The deal might set a precedent and could start a bidding war for artists between DreamWorks and other music companies. DreamWorks has already signed a distribution deal with MCA Music, who are in the process of improving their global distribution system.

Third, Michael Jackson's new compilation album of old and new material *HIStory* went straight to number one on the US music charts, only to be bumped down after three weeks by the soundtrack from *Pocahontas*, the Disney film. Sony is rumoured to have spent $30 million promoting the Jackson album and were hoping for better sales figures.

Fourth, in the largest deal in the history of the media, the Walt Disney Company acquired Capital Cities/ABC in a $19 billion merger that combined the legendary film company with the top ranked American TV network. The deal was announced the same week that the Disney soundtrack *Pocahontas* moved into the number one slot on the US music sales charts.

Disney have also indicated that they are interested in becoming a major player in the music industry. Other entertainment groups, including Viacom and 20th Century Fox have also announced that they are looking to diversify into the music business. EMI looks like the most probable acquisition candidate. The only thing one can predict with certainty is that the future will bring more change. Stay tuned.

Appendix

Internet World Wide Web (WWW) music home pages

The following WWW sites will get you started on the Internet. Most contain links to other interesting music sites. Please note that the sites vary in quality and tend to change rather often.

- *Internet Underground Music Archive*
  The coolest music site on the Internet.
  http://www.iuma.com/index.html

- *Music Resources on the Internet*
  If you can't find it here, maybe it doesn't exist.
  http://www.music.indiana.edu/misc/music-resources.html

- *Record Labels with World Wide Web Pages*
  The big and the small side by side.
  http://kzsu.stanford.edu/music/label-www.html

- *The International Association for the Study of Popular Music*
  IASPM is an international organization established to promote inquiry, scholarship and analysis in the area of popular music.
  http://xpress.comm.utulsa.edu/iaspm/iaspm.html

- *San Francisco Bay Area Underground Music*
  http://server.berkeley.edu/SFMusic/

- *Canadian Music Directory*
  A great link to artists, fanzines, record companies, music archives, etc.
  http://www.musical.net/imn/canada/index

- *The Canadian Music Exchange*
  Everything you always wanted to know about Canadian music.
  http://www.io.org/cme/

- *Sony*
  http://www.Sony.com/

- *Warner Music*
  http://www.iuma.com/warner/

- *Polygram*
  http://www.polygram.com/polygram/PolyGram.html

- *EMI*
  http://www.riv.nl/emi/default.html

- *MCA*
  http://www/mca.com/

- *Geffen/DGC*
  http://geffen.com/

- *Motown*
  http://www.musicbase.co.uk/music/motown/

- *Warner Music Sweden*
  http://www.ot.se/ot/wa-company-html

- *Sub pop*
  http://www.subpop.com/

- *National Academy of Recording Arts and Sciences*
  http://metavevse.com/grammy/

- *Internet Music Resource Guide*
  http://ww.teleport.com/~celinec/music.shtml

Bibliography

Adorno, T.W. (1941) 'On Popular Music', *Studies in Philosophy and Social Sciences*, 9: 17–48.

Adorno, T.W. (1972) *Introduction to the Sociology of Music*. New York: Seabury Press.

Allen, Robert (1987) *Channels of Discourse: Television and Contemporary Criticism*. London: Methuen.

Appadurai, Arjun (1990) 'Disjuncture and Difference in the Global Cultural Economy', in M. Featherstone (ed.), *Global Culture: Nationalism, Globalization and Modernity*. London: Sage.

Ash, Glen (1980) 'Community and Marketplace in Rock Music', MA thesis, Simon Fraser University.

Attali, Jacques (1985) *Noise: The Political Economy of Music*. Minneapolis: University of Minnesota Press.

Audley, Paul (1983) *Canada's Cultural Industries*. Toronto: Lorimer.

Bagdikian, Ben (1990) *The Media Monopoly*. Boston: Beacon Press.

Barbu, Z. (1976) 'Popular Culture: A Sociological Approach', pp. 39–68, in C.W.E. Bigsby (ed.), *Approaches to Popular Culture*. London: Arnold.

Barnes, Ken (1988) 'Top 40 Radio: A Fragment of the Imagination', pp. 8–50, in S. Frith (ed.), *Facing the Music*. New York: Pantheon.

Baskerville, David (1979) *Music Business Handbook*. Los Angeles: Sherwood.

Becker, Howard (1982) *Art Worlds*. Berkeley: University of California Press.

Beebe, J. (1977) 'Institutional Structure and Program Choices in Television Markets', *Quarterly Journal of Economics*, 12: 15–37.

Bell, Daniel (1965) *The End of Ideology*. New York: Collier-Macmillan.

Benjamin, Walter (1968) *Illuminations*. New York: Harcourt Press.

Berman, Marshall (1982) *All That Is Solid Melts into Air. The Experience of Modernity*. New York: Simon & Schuster.

Bernstein, C. (1990) 'The Leisure Empire', *Time*, 24 Dec., p. 57.

Biederman, D.E., E.P. Pierson, M.E. Silfen, J.A. Glasser and R.C. Berry (1992) *Law and Business of the Entertainment Industries*. New York: Praeger.

Billboard Chart Research. *Top Ten Pop Singles 1947–1989*.

Billboard Magazine. 1948–1994.

Blumler, Jay (1985) 'The Social Character of Media Gratifications', pp. 41–61, in K.E. Rosengren, L. Wenner and P. Palmgreen (eds), *Media Gratifications Research: Current Perspectives*. London: Sage.

Bourdieu, Pierre (1984) *Distinction: A Social Critique of the Judgement of Taste*. London: Routledge & Kegan Paul.

Bourdieu, P. and J.-C. Passeron (1977) *Reproduction in Education, Society and Culture*. London: Sage.

Box, G. and G. Jenkins (1976) *Time Series Analysis: Forecasting and Control*. San Francisco: Holden Day.

Bradley, Dick (1981) 'Music and Social Science: A Survey', *Media, Culture and Society*, 3: 205–218.

Brake, Mike (1980) *The Sociology of Youth and Youth Subcultures*. London: Routledge & Kegan Paul.

Brolinson, P.E. and H. Larsen (1981) *Rock*. Stockholm: Esselte Studium.

Brolinson, P.E. and H. Larsen (1984) *När rocken slog i Sverige*. Stockholm: Sweden Music.

Brunner, Ronald and Gary Brewer (1971) *Organized Complexity*. New York: The Free Press.

Burnett, Robert (1987) 'The Global Jukebox?', pp. 147–155, in U. Carlsson (ed.), *Forskning om populärkultur*. Gothenburg: NORDICOM.

Burnett, Robert (1988a) 'Economic Aspects of the Phonogram Industry', pp. 112–126, in U. Carlsson (ed.), *Ekonomiska Perspektiv i Forskning om Massmedier*. Gothenburg: NORDICOM.

Burnett, Robert (1988b) 'Musikvanor i Sverige', pp. 59–62, in S. Holmberg and L. Weibull (eds), *Samhälle Opinion Massmedia 1987*. Department of Political Science and Unit of Mass Communication, University of Gothenburg.

Burnett, Robert (1989) 'Musik för Miljoner', *Tvärsnitt*, 11: 18–23.

Burnett, Robert (1990a) 'Concentration and Diversity in the International Phonogram Industry', Ph.D. dissertation, Gothenburg Studies in Journalism and Mass Communication, University of Gothenburg.

Burnett, Robert (1990b) 'From a Whisper to a Scream: Music Video and Cultural Form', pp. 21–29, in K. Roe and U. Carlsson (eds), *Popular Music Research in Sweden*. Gothenburg: NORDICOM.

Burnett, Robert (1992a) 'Dressed for Success: Sweden from Abba to Roxette', *Popular Music*, 11: 141–149.

Burnett, Robert (1992b) 'The Implications of Ownership Changes on Concentration and Diversity in the Phonogram Industry', *Communication Research*, 19: 749–769.

Burnett, Robert (1993) 'The Popular Music Industry in Transition', *Popular Music and Society*, 17: 91–118.

Burnett, Robert and Robert Philip Weber (1989) 'Concentration and Diversity in the Popular Music Industry 1948–1986', competitive paper presented at 84th Annual American Sociological Association Conference, San Francisco.

Cantor, Muriel (1980) *Prime Time Television: Content and Control*. Beverly Hills: Sage.

Carey, James (1983) 'The Origins of Radical Discourse on Cultural Studies in the United States', *Journal of Communication*, 33: 311–314.

Carey, James (1989) *Communication as Culture*. Boston: Unwin Hyman.

Carroll, Glenn (1984) 'Organizational Ecology', *Annual Review of Sociology*, 10: 71–93.

Carroll, Glenn (1985) 'Concentration and Specialization: Dynamics of Niche Width in Populations of Organizations', *American Journal of Sociology*, 90: 1262–1283.

Castro, Janice (1990) 'Let Us Entertain You', *Time*, 10 Dec., p. 52.

Chaffee, Steven (1985) 'Popular Music and Communication Research', *Communication Research*, 12: 413–424.

Chambers, Iain (1982) 'Some Critical Tracks', *Popular Music*, 2: 19–36.

Chapple, Steve and Reebee Garofalo (1977) *Rock 'n' Roll is Here to Pay*. Chicago: Nelson Hall.

Chesebro, J., D. Foulger, J. Nachman and A. Yannelli (1985) 'Popular Music as a Mode of Communication, 1955–1982', *Critical Studies in Mass Communication*, 2: 115–135.

Clarinews/UPI (1993) 'Murdoch Unveils Plans to Expand Global Communications Empire', 2 Sept.

Clarinews/UPI (1993) 'Bertlesmann Planning CD-ROM Music Label', 10 Sept.

Clarinews/UPI (1993) 'Viacom and Paramount Merger', 13 Sept.

Clarinews/UPI (1993) 'Time Warner Closes US West Deal', 15 Sept.

Clarinews/UPI (1993) 'Sony, Blockbuster, Pace Teaming Up', 1 Nov.

Clarinews/UPI (1993) 'MGM Signs Distribution Deal with Polygram', 1 Nov.

Clarinews/UPI (1993) 'Cap Cities to Acquire 21 per cent Stake in Scandinavian Broadcasting', 16 Nov.

Clarinews/UPI (1993) 'Time Warner Sets Interactive News-On-Demand Service', 16 Nov.

Coser, Lewis, Charles Kadushin and Walter Powell (1982) *Books: The Culture and Commerce of Publishing*. Chicago: University of Chicago Press.

Dannen, Fredric (1990) *Hit Men*. New York: Random House.

DeFleur, M. and S. Ball-Rokeach (1988) *Theories of Mass Communication*. New York: Longman.

Denisoff, R. Serge (1975) *Solid Gold: The Popular Record Industry*. New Brunswick: Transaction.

Denisoff, R. Serge (1986) *Tarnished Gold: The Record Industry Revisited*. New Brunswick: Transaction.

Denisoff, R. Serge (1988) *Inside MTV*. New Brunswick: Transaction.

Denisoff, R. Serge and Mark Levine (1970) 'Generations and Counter-Culture: A Study in the Ideology of Music', *Youth and Society*, 12: 33–58.

Denski, Stan (1989) 'One Step Up and Two Steps Back: A Heuristic Model for Popular Music and Communication Research', *Popular Music and Society*, 13: 9–21.

Details (1994) 'Totally Wired', July, p. 121.

DiMaggio, Paul (1977) 'Market Structure, the Creative Process, and Popular Culture', *Journal of Popular Culture*, 11: 436–452.

DiMaggio, Paul (1987) 'Classification in Art', *American Sociological Review*, 52: 440–455.

DiMaggio, Paul and Paul Hirsch (1976) 'Production Organization in the Arts', *American Behavioral Scientist*, 19: 735–749.

Dimmick, John (1986) 'Sociocultural Evolution in the Communication Industries', *Communication Research*, 13: 473–508.

Dimmick, J. and E. Rothenbuhler (1984) 'The Theory of the Niche: Quantifying Competition among Media Industries', *Journal of Communication*, 34: 103–119.

Dominick, John and Mark Pierce (1976) 'Trends in Network Prime-time Programming, 1953–1974', *Journal of Communication*, 26: 70–80.

Durant, Alan (1984) *Conditions of Music*. London: Macmillan.

Eberly, Phillip (1982) *Music in the Air*. New York: Hastings House.

Economist (1990) 'Janus of the Turntable', 11 Aug.

Eliot, Marc (1990) *Rockonomics: The Money Behind the Music*. New York: Omnibus.

Elliot, Dave (1982) 'The Rock Music Industry', *Science, Technology and Popular Culture (1)*. Milton Keynes: Open University Press.

Enzenberger, Hans Magnus (1970) 'Constituents of a Theory of the Media', *New Left Review*, 64: 13–36.

Enzenberger, Hans Magnus (1974) *The Consciousness Industry*. New York: Seabury Press.

Ernsberger, Richard (1992) 'Europe's Ailing Giant', *Newsweek*, 5 Oct., p. 42.

Ettema, J., D. Whitney and D. Wackman (1987) 'Professional Mass Communicators', pp. 747–780, in C. Berger and S. Chaffee (eds), *Handbook of Communication Science*. London: Sage.

European (1994) 'Copyright Is the Key for Viacom', 21 Oct., p. 19.

Ewen, Stuart (1983) 'The Implications of Empiricism', *Journal of Communication*, 3: 219–225.

Feihl, John (1981) *Music Trends: Characteristics of the Billboard Charts, 1955–1977*. Ottawa: Canadian Radio-television and Telecommunications Commission.

Fejes, Fred (1981) 'Media Imperialism: An Assessment', *Media, Culture and Society*, 3: 281–289.

Financial Times (1989) 'Time Warner Deal Takes US Back to the Future', 6 March.

Financial Times (1990) 'Time Warner's Global Strategy', 10 April.

Fish, Stanley (1980) *Is There a Text in This Class?* New York: Cambridge University Press.

Fisher, Franklin (1961) 'On the Cost of Approximate Specification in Simultaneous Equation Estimation', *Econometrica*, 29: 139–170.

Fiske, John (1987) *Television Culture*. London: Methuen.

Fiske, John (1989) *Understanding Popular Culture*. Boston: Unwin Hyman.

Fornäs, J., U. Lindberg and O. Sernhede (1988) *Under rocken. Musikens roll i tre unga band*. Stockholm: Symposium.

Fox, Ted (1986) *In the Groove*. New York: St Martin's Press.

Freeman, John (1983) 'Granger Causality and the Time Series Analysis of Political Relationships', *American Journal of Political Science*, 27: 327–358.

Frith, Simon (1978) *The Sociology of Rock*. London: Constable.

Frith, Simon (1981) *Sound Effects*. New York: Pantheon.

Frith, Simon (1986a) 'Hearing Secret Harmonies', pp. 53–70, in C. MacCabe (ed.), *High Theory/Low Culture*. New York: St Martin's Press.

Frith, Simon (1986b) 'Art vs. Technology', *Media, Culture and Society*, 8: 263–279.

Frith, Simon (1987) 'Music and Copyright', *Popular Music*, 7: 53–75.

Frith, Simon (1988a) *Music for Pleasure*. Cambridge: Polity Press.

Frith, Simon (ed.) (1988b) *Facing the Music*. New York: Pantheon.

Frith, Simon (ed.) (1989) *World Music, Politics and Social Change*. Manchester: Manchester University Press.

Frith, Simon (1991) 'Anglo-America and its Discontents', *Cultural Studies*, 15: 263–269.

Frith, Simon and Andrew Goodwin (eds) (1990) *On Record*. New York: Pantheon.

Frith, Simon and Howard Horne (1987) *Art into Pop*. London: Methuen.

Gans, Herbert (1974) *Popular Culture and High Culture*. New York: Basic Books.

Garcia, Guy (1991) 'Play It Again, Sampler'. *Time*, 3 June, p. 60.

Garnham, Nicholas (1987) 'Concepts of Culture: Public Policy and the Cultural Industries', *Cultural Studies*, 1: 1, 23–37.

Gelatt, Roland (1977) *The Fabulous Phonograph: 1877–1977*. New York: Collier.

Gelman, M. (1990) 'Valenti Spurs Pols to Keep US Showbox in GATT Gab', *Variety*, 12 Nov., p. 12.

Giddens, Anthony (1990) *The Consequences of Modernity*. Stanford: Stanford University Press.

Gillett, Charlie (1972) *The Sound of the City*. New York: Dell.

Gitlin, Todd (1978) 'Media Sociology: The Dominant Paradigm', *Theory and Society*, 7: 205–253.

Gitlin, Todd (1981) 'Television Screens: Hegemony in Transition', in M. Apple (ed.), *Cultural and Economic Reproduction in Education*. London: Routledge & Kegan Paul.

Gitlin, Todd (1985) *Watching Television*. New York: Pantheon.

Glassman, R.B. (1973) 'Persistence and Loose Coupling in Living Systems', *Behavioral Science*, 18: 83–98.

GLF (1989–92) *Musik på Fonogram*. Solna: Sweden.

Goodman, Fred (1991) 'Who Do You Blow?', *Voice*, 6 Aug., p. 41.

Goodman, Fred (1992) 'Big Deals', *Musician*, 1 Jan., p. 51.

Goodwin, Andrew (1986) 'Introduction', *Media, Culture and Society*, 8: 1–3.

Goodwin, Andrew (1992) *Dancing in the Distraction Factory*. Minneapolis: University of Minnesota Press.

Gottlieb, Anthony (1991) 'Almost Grown: A Survey of the Music Business', *Economist*, 21 Dec., pp. 1–18.

Gottman, John (1981) *Time-Series Analysis: A Comprehensive Introduction for Social Scientists*. Cambridge: Cambridge University Press.

Granger, C.W.J. and Paul Newbold (1977) *Forecasting Economic Time Series*. New York: Academic Press.

Gronow, Pekka (1977) 'Structuring Diverse Tastes', pp. 59–64, in Cees Hamelink (ed.), *The Corporate Village*. Rome: IDOC.

Gronow, Pekka (1980) *Statistics in the Field of Sound Recordings*. Division of Statistics on Culture and Communication, report c-21. Paris: UNESCO.

Gronow, Pekka (1983) 'The Record Industry: The Growth of a Mass Medium', *Popular Music*, 3: 53–77.

Guback, Thomas (1969) *The International Film Industry*. Bloomington: Indiana University Press.

Guback, Thomas (1982) 'Theatrical Films', pp. 199–298, in B. Compaine, C. Sterling, T. Guback and J. Noble (eds), *Who Owns the Media? Concentration of Ownership in the Mass Communications Industry*. New York: Knowledge.

Guback, Thomas and Tapio Varis (1982) *Transnational Communication and Cultural Industries*. Paris: UNESCO.

Gustafsson, Karl Erik (1988) 'Ekonomiskt inriktad forskning om massmedier. En introduktion', pp. 9–13, in Ulla Carlsson (ed.), *Ekonomiska Perspektiv i Forskning om Massmedier*. Gothenburg: NORDICOM.

Hall, Stuart (1980) 'Cultural Studies: Two Paradigms', *Media, Culture and Society*, 3: 57–72.

Hall, Stuart and Paddy Whannel (1964) *The Popular Arts*. London: Hutchinson.

Hamelink, Cees (1983) *Finance and Information*. New Jersey: Ablex.

Hannan, Michael and John Freeman (1988) 'The Population Ecology of Organizations', *American Journal of Sociology*, 82: 929–962.

Hardy, Phil (1985) *The British Record Industry*. IASPM-UK Working Paper 3.

Harker, Dave (1980) *One for the Money: Politics and Popular Song*. London: Hutchinson.

Harvey, David (1989) *The Condition of Postmodernity*. Oxford: Basil Blackwell.

Hebdige, Dick (1979) *Subculture: The Meaning of Style*. London: Methuen.

Hebdige, Dick (1987) *Cut 'N' Mix*. London: Comedia.

Hebdige, Dick (1988) *Hiding in the Light*. London: Routledge.

Hellman, Heiki (1983) 'The New State of Competition in the Record Industry', *Sociologia*, 20: 355–367.

Hellman, Heiki (1985) 'Från cykel till symbios', *NordNytt*, 24: 35–43.

Hellman, H. and M. Soramäki (1994) 'Competition and Content in the US Video Market', *Journal of Media Economics*, 7: 29–49.

Hennion, A. (1983) 'The Production of Success: An Anti-musicology of the Pop Song', *Popular Music*, 3: 159–193.

Hesbacher, P., R. Downing and D. Berger (1975) 'Record Roulette: What Makes It Spin?', *Journal of Communication*, 25: 74–85.

Hibbs, Douglas Jr (1977) 'On Analyzing the Effects of Policy Interventions: Box-Tiao vs. Structural Equation Models', pp. 167–186, in H. Costner (ed.), *Sociological Methodology*. San Francisco: Jossey-Bass.

Hirsch, Paul (1970) *The Structure of the Popular Music Industry*. Survey Research Center, Ann Arbor: University of Michigan.

Hirsch, Paul (1972) 'Processing Fads and Fashions: An Organizational Set Analysis of Cultural Industry Systems', *American Journal of Sociology*, 77: 639–659.

Hirsch, Paul (1977) 'Occupational, Organizational, and Institutional Models in Mass Media Research: Towards an Integrated Framework', pp. 13–43, in P. Hirsch, P. Miller and F. Kline (eds), *Strategies for Communication Research*: Sage Annual Reviews of Communication Research. Beverly Hills: Sage.

Hirsch, Paul (1978) 'Production and Distribution Roles among Cultural Organizations', *Social Research*, 45: 315–330.

Hopkins, T. and I. Wallerstein (1982) *World Systems Analysis: Theory and Methodology*. Beverly Hills: Sage.

Horkheimer, Max and Theodor W. Adorno (1972) *Dialectic of Enlightenment*. New York: Seabury.

IFPI. International Federation of Phonogram and Videogram Producers. Annual Reports and Newsletter.

IFPI (1995) 'IFPI in 1995', *For the Record*, p. 1.

Innis, Harold Adams (1950) *Empire and Communication*. Toronto: University of Toronto Press.

Innis, Harold Adams (1951) *The Bias of Communication*. Toronto: University of Toronto Press.

Jameson, Frederic (1984) 'Postmodernism, or the Cultural Logic of Late Capitalism', *New Left Review*, 146: 53–92.

Jensen, Joli (1984) 'An Interpretive Approach to Culture Production', pp. 99–118, in W. Rowland and B. Watkins (eds), *Interpreting Television: Current Research Perspectives*. Beverly Hills: Sage.

Jowett, Garth and James Linton (1980) *Movies as Mass Communication*. Beverly Hills: Sage.

Kaplan, E. Ann (1987) *Rocking around the Clock*. New York: Methuen.

Kapp, M., M. Middlestat and M. Fishbein (1982) *Home Taping: A Consumer Survey*. New York: Warner Communications Ltd.

Katz, Elihu and George Wedell (1977) *Broadcasting in the Third World: Promise and Performance*. Cambridge: Harvard University Press.

Kay, Helen (1993) 'Music Played on a Major Scale', *The Independent*, 8 Aug., p. 6.

Kealy, Edward (1982) 'Conventions and the Production of the Popular Music Aesthetic', *Journal of Popular Culture*, 16: 100–115.

King, Mike (1977) 'Popular Culture in Cross-Cultural Perspective', *Topics in Cultural Learning*, 5: 83–91.

Koval, Howard (1988) 'Homogenization of Culture in Capitalist Society', *Popular Music and Society*, 12: 1–16.

Kroeber, Arthur and Clyde Kluckhohn (1952) *Culture: A Critical Review of Concepts and Definitions*. Harvard University Peabody Museum of American Archeology and Ethnology Papers, 47.

Laing, Dave (1985) *One Chord Wonders*. Milton Keynes: Open University Press.

Laing, Dave (1986) 'The Music Industry and the Cultural Imperialism Thesis', *Media, Culture and Society*, 8: 331–341.

Landler, Mark (1993) 'Now EMI is Really Rocking', *Business Week*, 23 Aug., p. 31.

Lazarsfeld, Paul (1941) 'Remarks on Administrative and Critical Communications Research', in Max Horkheimer (ed.), *Studies in Philosophy and Social Science*, 9: 2–16.

Lazarsfeld, Paul and Frank Stanton (eds) (1941) *Radio Research, 1941*. New York: Arno.

Lazarsfeld, Paul and Frank Stanton (eds) (1944) *Radio Research, 1942–1943*. New York: Arno.

Lazarsfeld, Paul and Frank Stanton (eds) (1949) *Communications Research, 1948–1949*. New York: Arno.

Lee, C.C. (1980) *Media Imperialism Reconsidered: The Homogenizing of Television Culture*. Beverly Hills: Sage.

Lewis, George (1978) 'The Sociology of Popular Culture', *Current Sociology*, 26: 1–122.

Lopes, Paul (1992) 'Innovation and Diversity in the Popular Music Industry, 1969–1990', *American Sociological Review*, 57: 56–71.

Lull, James (ed.) (1987) *Popular Music and Communication*. London: Sage.

Luyken, George (1986) 'Pan-European Television', *Media Bulletin*, 3: 3–4.

Malm, Krister (1982) 'Phonograms and Cultural Policy in Sweden', pp. 43–75, in Kurt Blaukopf (ed.), *The Phonogram in Cultural Communication*. Vienna: Springer.

March, J.G. and J.P. Olsen (1976) *Ambiguity and Choice in Organizations*. Bergen: Universitetsforlaget.

Marcuse, Herbert (1964) *One-Dimensional Man*. Boston: Beacon Press.

Mattelart, Armand (1979) *Multinational Corporations and the Control of Culture*. Sussex: Harvester Press.

Mattelart, Armand (1984) *International Image Markets: In Search of an Alternative Perspective*. London: Comedia.

McAnany, Emile (1985) 'Cultural Industries in International Perspective: Convergence or Conflict?', pp. 1–29, in B. Dervin and M. Voigt (eds), *Progress in Communication Sciences*, 6. New Jersey: Ablex.

McCleary, Richard and Richard Hay (1980) *Applied Time Series Analysis for the Social Sciences*. Beverly Hills: Sage.

McLuhan, Marshall (1965) *Understanding Media: The Extensions of Man*. New York: McGraw-Hill.

McLuhan, Marshall and Quentin Fiore (1967) *The Medium is the Massage*. New York: Bantam.

McPhee, William (1966) 'When Culture Becomes a Business', in J. Berger, M. Zelditch and B. Anderson (eds), *Sociological Theories in Progress*, 1. New York: Houghton Mifflin.

McQuail, Denis (1986) 'Commercialization', pp. 152–178, in Denis McQuail and Karen Siune (eds), *New Media Politics*. London: Sage.

McQuail, Denis (1987) *Mass Communication Theory*. London: Sage.

Melly, George (1972) *Revolt into Style*. London: Penguin.

Meyer, John and Brian Rowan (1978) 'The Structure of Educational Organizations', pp. 78–109, in M. Meyer (ed.), *Environments and Organizations*. San Francisco: Jossey Bass.

Mondak, Jeffrey (1989) 'Cultural Heterogeneity in Capitalist Society: In Defense of Repetition on the Billboard Hot 100', *Popular Music and Society*, 13: 45–58.

Mowlana, H. (1986) *Global Information and World Communication*. London: Longman.

Muikku, Jari (1987) *Gone with the Vinyl*. Helsinki: Institute of Workers' Music.

Murdock, Graham (1982) 'Large Corporations and the Control of the Communications Industries', pp. 118–150, in M. Gurevitch, T. Bennett, J. Curran and J. Woollacott (eds), *Culture, Society and the Media*. New York: Methuen.

Nader, Ralph (1993) personal memorandum, 19 Oct.

Neff, Robert (1992) 'Sony's Recipe: One Part Hardware, One Part Software', *Business Week*, 7 Sept.

Negus, Keith (1992) *Producing Pop*. London: Edward Arnold.

Nelson, Joyce (1979) 'TV Pleasure Centers', *In Search*, 8: 16–25.

New York Times (1993) 'Microsoft and 2 Cable Giants Close to an Alliance', 5 July.

New York Times (1993) 'Clinton Hails Breakthrough', 14 Dec.

Norberg, Jan and Göran Nylöf (1988) *Kulturbarometern i detalj: Tema Musik*. SR/PUB-Statens Kulturråd.

Nord, David P. (1980) 'An Economic Perspective on Formula in Popular Culture', *Journal of American Culture*, 3: 17–31.

Nordenstreng, Kaarle and Herbert Schiller (1979) *National Sovereignty and International Communication*. New Jersey: Ablex.

Nordenstreng, Kaarle and Tapio Varis (1974) *Television Traffic – a One-Way Street?* Reports and papers on mass Communication, 70. Paris: UNESCO.

Nye, Russell (1970) *The Unembarrassed Muse: The Popular Arts in America*. New York: Dial Press.

Ouchi, William (1978) 'Coupled versus Uncoupled Control in Organizational Hierarchies', pp. 264–289, in M. Meyer (ed.), *Environments and Organizations*. San Francisco: Jossey Bass.

Pareles, Jon. (1990) 'The Big Get Bigger', *New York Times*, 19 March, p. 3.

Pareles, Jon. (1991) 'As MTV Turns 10, Pop Goes the World', *New York Times*, 7 July, p. 1.

Peacock, Alan and Ronald Weir (1975) *The Composer in the Marketplace*. London: Faber.

Pearsall, Ronald (1973) *Victorian Popular Music*. Newton Abbot: David & Charles.

Perrow, Charles (1986) *Complex Organizations*. New York: Random House.

Peterson, Richard (1976) 'The Production of Culture: A Prolegomenon', pp. 7–22, in R. Peterson (ed.), *The Production of Culture*. Beverly Hills: Sage.

Peterson, Richard (1979) 'Revitalizing the Culture Concept', *Annual Review of Sociology*, 5: 137–166.

Peterson, Richard (1982) 'Five Constraints on the Production of Culture: Law, Technology, Market, Organizational Structure and Occupational Careers', *Journal of Popular Culture*, 16: 158–173.

Peterson, Richard (1985) 'Six Constraints on the Production of Literary Works', *Poetics*, 14: 45–67.

Peterson, Richard and David Berger (1971) 'Entrepreneurship in Organizations: Evidence from the Popular Music Industry', *Administrative Science Quarterly*, 16: 97–107.

Peterson, Richard and David Berger (1975) 'Cycles in Symbol Production: The Case of Popular Music', *American Sociological Review*, 40: 158–173.

Peterson, Richard and Paul DiMaggio (1975) 'From Region to Class, the Changing Locus of Country Music', *Social Forces*, 53: 497–506.

Peterson, Richard and Michael Hughes (1984) 'Isolating Patterns of Cultural Choice to Facilitate the Formation of Cultural Indicators', pp. 443–452, in G. Melischek, K.E. Rosengren and J. Stappers (eds), *Cultural Indicators: An International Symposium*. Vienna: Austrian Academy of Science.

Peterson, Richard and Howard White (1979) 'The Simplex Located in Art Worlds', *Urban Life*, 7: 411–439.

Peterson, Richard and Howard White (1981) 'Elements of Simplex Structure', *Urban Life*, 10: 3–24.

Porter, Michael (1980) *Competitive Strategy*. New York: Free Press.

Powell, Walter (1985) *Getting Into Print*. Chicago: University of Chicago Press.

Qualen, John (1985) *The Music Industry: The End of Vinyl?* London: Comedia.

Radway, Janice (1984) *Reading the Romance: Women, Patriarchy, and Popular Literature*. Chapel Hill: University of North Carolina Press.

Real, Michael (1977) *Mass Mediated Culture*. Englewood Cliffs: Prentice-Hall.

Reyes Matta, Fernando (1982) 'Popular Song, the Recording Industry, and Their Alternative Facets', *Media Development*, 1: 12–20.

RIAA (1985–92) *Inside the Recording Industry: A Statistical Overview*. New York: Recording Industry Association of America.

RIAA. Recording Industry Association of America, Annual Reports.

Rieger, Jon (1975) 'The Coming Crisis in the Youth Music Market', *Popular Music and Society*, 4: 19–35.

Riesman, David (1950) 'Listening to Popular Music', *American Quarterly*, 2: 359–371.

Riesman, David (1951) *The Lonely Crowd*. New Haven: Yale University Press.

Robinson, Deanna C. (1986) 'Youth and Popular Music: A Theoretical Rationale for an International Study', *Gazette*, 37: 33–50.

Roe, Keith (1983) *Mass Media and Adolescent Schooling: Co-existence or Conflict?* Stockholm: Almqvist and Wiksell International.

Roe, Keith (1985) *The Programme Output of Seven Cable-TV Channels: A Descriptive Analysis*. Dept of Sociology, University of Lund.

Roe, Keith (1985) 'Introduction', *Communication Research*, 12: 275–276.

Roe, Keith and U. Johnsson-Smaragdi (1987) 'The Swedish "Mediascape" in the 1980s', *European Journal of Communication*, 2: 357–370.

Roe, Keith and M. Löfgren (1988) 'Music Video Use and Educational Achievement', *Popular Music*, 7: 303–314.

Roe, Keith and R. Wallis (1989) 'One Planet – One Music: The Development of Music Television in Western Europe', *Nordicom Review*, 1: 35–40.

Rogers, Everett and Rekhal Rogers (1976) *Communication in Organizations*. New York: Free Press.

Rosengren, Karl Erik (1983) *The Climate of Literature*. Lund: Studentlitteratur.

Rosengren, Karl Erik (1983) 'Communication Research: One Paradigm or Four?', *Journal of Communication*, 33: 185–207.

Rosengren, Karl Erik (1985) 'Culture, Media and Society', *Massacommunicatie*, 13: 126–144.

Rosmarin, Adena (1985) *The Power of Genre*. Minneapolis: University of Minnesota Press.

Rothenbuhler, Eric and John Dimmick (1982) 'Popular Music: Concentration and Diversity in the Industry, 1974–1980', *Journal of Communication*, 32: 143–149.

Rowland, Willard D. Jr (1983) *The Politics of TV Violence: Policy Uses of Communication Research*. Beverly Hills: Sage.

Rutten, Paul (1991) 'Local Popular Music on the National and International Markets', *Cultural Studies*, October: 294–305.

Ryan, John (1985) *The Production of Culture in the Music Industry*. New York: New York University Press.

Ryan, John and Richard Peterson (1982) 'The Product Image: The Fate of Creativity in Country Music Songwriting', *Sage Annual Reviews of Communication Research*, 10: 11–32.

Sánchez-Tabernero, A. (1993) *Media Concentration in Europe*. Manchester: The European Institute for the Media.

Scherer, Fredrick (1970/1980) *Industrial Market Structure and Economic Performance*. Chicago: Rand McNally.

Schiller, Herbert (1969) *Mass Communication and American Empire*. Boston: Beacon.

Schiller, Herbert (1976) *Communication and Cultural Domination*. New York: International Arts and Sciences.

Schiller, Herbert (1981) *Who Knows? Information in the Age of the Fortune 500*. New Jersey: Ablex.

Schiller, Herbert (1984) *Information and the Crisis Economy*. New Jersey: Ablex.

Schiller, Herbert (1989) *Culture, Inc.: The Corporate Takeover of Public Expression*. New York: Oxford University Press.

Schlender, Brenton (1992) 'How Sony Keeps the Magic Going', *Fortune*, 24 Feb.

Schöld, Eva and Margareta Wikström (1989) *Musik På Fonogram*. Stockholm: Statens Kulturråd.

Schumpeter, John (1950) *Capitalism, Socialism and Democracy*. New York: Harper & Row.

Shadbolt, Peter (1993) 'George Michael Takes on the Might of Sony', *Clarinews/ UPI*, 18 Sept.

Shemel, Sidney and William Krasilovsky (1979) *This Business of Music*. New York: Billboard.

Shils, Edward (1961) 'The Mass Society and Its Culture', in N. Jacobs (ed.), *Culture for the Millions*. Princeton: Van Nostrand.

Shore, Lawrence (1983) 'The Crossroads of Business and Music: The Music Industry in the US and Internationally', Ph.D. dissertation, Stanford University.

Simon, Herbert (1981) *The Sciences of the Artificial*. Cambridge: MIT Press.

Simon, Herbert and Albert Ando (1961) 'Aggregation of Variables in Dynamic Systems', *Econometrica*, 29: 111–138.

Sinclair, John (1992) 'Media and Cultural Industries: An Overview', *CIRCIT Newsletter*, Aug., pp. 3–4.

Singer, Mark (1968) 'The Concept of Culture', *International Encyclopedia of the Social Sciences*, 3: 527–543.

Smith, Anthony (1980) *The Geopolitics of Information*. New York: Oxford.

Smythe, Dallas (1981) *Dependency Road: Communications, Capitalism, Consciousness and Canada*. New Jersey: Ablex.

Soocher, Stan (1993) 'George Michael vs. Sony', *Musician*, 1 Feb., p. 34.

Soramäki, Matti and Jari Haarma (1981) *The International Music Industry*. Helsinki: The Finnish Broadcasting Company.

Statens Kulturråd (1989) *Musik på Fonogram*. Stockholm.

Steele, Lowell (1975) *Innovation in Big Business*. New York: Elsevier.

Stokes, Geoffrey (1977) *Star Making Machinery*. New York: Vantage.

Swingewood, Allan (1977) *The Myth of Mass Culture*. London: Macmillan.

Tagg, Philip (1982) 'Analysing Popular Music: Theory, Method and Practice', *Popular Music*, 2: 37–69.

Tagg, Philip (1987) 'Musicology and the Semiotics of Popular Music', *Semiotica*, 66: 279–298.

Tahmincioglu, Eve (1993) 'Sony Names Schulhof Head of Electronics and Entertainment Units', *Clarinews/UPI*, 24 May.

Tracey, Michael (1985) 'The Poisoned Chalice? International Television and the Idea of Dominance', *Daedalus*, 15: 17–56.

Tremlett, George (1990) *Rock Gold: The Music Millionaires*. London: Unwin Hyman.

Truzzi, Mark (1977) 'Towards a General Sociology of the Folk, Popular and Elite Arts', pp. 279–289, in R. Jones (ed.), *Research in Sociology of Knowledge, Sciences and Art*. Greenwich: JAI Press.

Tsiantar, D. and J. Hammer (1992) 'Risqué Business at Time Warner', *Newsweek*, 2 Nov., p. 45.

Tuchman, Gaye (1983) 'Consciousness Industries and the Production of Culture', *Journal of Communications*, 33: 330–341.

Tugendhat, Carl (1973) *The Multinationals*. Harmondsworth: Penguin.

Tunstall, Jeremy (1977) *The Media Are American*. New York: Columbia University Press.

Tunstall, Jeremy (1986) *Communications Deregulations*. New York: Basil Blackwell.

Turow, Joseph (1991) 'A Mass Communication Perspective on Entertainment Industries', in J. Curran and M. Gurevitch (eds), *Mass Media and Society*. New York: Routledge.

Turow, Joseph (1992) *Media Systems in Society*. New York: Longman.

Turow, Joseph (1992) 'The Organizational Underpinnings of Contemporary Media Conglomerates', *Communication Research*, 19: 682–704.

UNESCO (1982) *A Challenge of the Future of Culture*. Paris: UNESCO.

Variety (1983) 'MTV Overtaking Radio as Motivation of Disc Purchases', 16 Feb., p. 113.

Variety (1988) 'MCA Acquires Motown', 24 Nov.

Varis, Tapio (1973) *International Inventory of Television Programme Structure and the Flow of TV Programmes between Nations*. University of Tampere: Institute of Journalism and Mass Communication, Report No. 20.

Varis, Tapio (1984) 'The International Flow of Television Programs', *Journal of Communication*, 32: 143–152.

Varis, Tapio (1985) 'International Flow of Television Programs', Reports and papers on Mass Communication, No. 100, Paris: UNESCO.

Vogel, Harold (1986) *Entertainment Industry Economics: A Guide for Financial Analysis*. Cambridge: Cambridge University Press.

Wallerstein, Immanuel (1975) *The Modern World System*. New York: Academic Press.

Wallis, Roger (1991) 'Internationalisation, Localisation, and Integration', Ph.D. dissertation, University of Gothenburg.

Wallis, Roger and Krister Malm (1984) *Big Sounds from Small Peoples*. London: Constable.

Wallis, Roger and Krister Malm (1992) *Media Policy and Music Activity*. London: Routledge.

Wasko, Janet (1982) *Movies and Money: Financing the American Film Industry*. New Jersey: Ablex.

Weber, Robert Philip (1982) 'The Long-term Problem Solving Dynamics of Social Systems', *European Journal of Political Research*, 10: 387–405.

Weber, Robert Philip (1987) 'Cycles of the Third Kind', *European Journal of Political Research*, 15: 263–275.

Weber, William (1977) 'Mass Culture and the Reshaping of European Musical Taste', *International Review of the Aesthetics and Sociology of Music*, 8.

Weick, Karl (1976) 'Educational Organizations as Loosely Coupled Systems', *Administrative Science Quarterly*, 21: 1–19.

Whitburn, Joel (1988) *Top 40 Hits*. New York: Guinness.

Wicke, Peter (1984) 'Young People and Popular Music in the GDR', Paper presented to the International Association for Mass Communication Research Conference, Prague, 1984.

Wicke, Peter (1990) *Rock Music: Culture, Aesthetics and Sociology*. Cambridge: Cambridge University Press.

Williams, Raymond (1961) *The Long Revolution*. London: Chatto & Windus.

Williams, Raymond (1975) *Television: Technology and Cultural Form*. New York: Schocken Books.

Williams, Raymond (1976) *Keywords*. London: Fontana.

Williams, Raymond (1981) *Culture*. London: Fontana.

Willis, Paul (1978) *Profane Culture*. London: Routledge & Kegan Paul.

Willis, Paul (1990) *Common Culture*. London: Routledge.

Wired (1994a) 'The Future of CDs', p. 60.

Wired (1994b) 'Consume the Minimum, Produce the Maximum', p. 114.

Wolff, Janet (1981) *The Social Production of Art*. New York: St Martin's.

Index